[Y2K is] one of the most serious and potentially devastating events this nation has ever encountered. . . . This problem will affect us all individually and collectively in very profound ways.

—U.S. Senate Special Committee on the Year 2000 Technology Problem, February 25, 1999

101 WAYS TO SURVIVE

the Y2K Crisis

S. F. Tomajczyk

St. Martin's Griffin ⚏ New York

ISBN 0-312-24591-2

First St. Martin's Griffin Edition: May 1999

Text design by Stanley S. Drate / Folio Graphics Co. Inc.

10 9 8 7 6 5 4 3 2

Dedicated to
the special people in my life who
taught me to always
Be Prepared

For Joyce

Contents

Acknowledgments

I wish to extend my special and warmhearted thanks to my literary agent, Laura Tucker, at Richard Curtis Associates, and to my editor, Barry Neville, at St. Martin's Press. This book would not have been "born" without their insight, involvement, and unfailing support.

Introduction

We live in an unpredictable and oftentimes violent world. Whether it's natural disasters like floods and earthquakes or man-made emergencies like hazardous chemical spills and terrorist attacks, we live hand in hand with these forces and come to accept them, adapting to their rude arrival and cheering their slow but inevitable departure.

The Year 2000 problem—referred to as "Y2K" by many, "the great computer glitch" by some, and the "millennium bug" by still others—is simply another thing we have to confront and deal with as being part of our society. We may not like it. We may be frightened by its possible consequences. And we may even be angry at it for forcing us to focus our attention and efforts elsewhere.

Yet, like it or not, it is here. Y2K is a problem that we created for ourselves, and now we must deal with it. Hopefully, we will also overcome it.

People who know me know that I'm a fairly intelligent, open-minded, and level-headed person. I had to be. Why? For eight years I served as the spokesperson for my state's Health Department. That meant I was involved in the best and the worst of things.

Severe weather.

Disease outbreaks.

Radiation hazards.

Water quality.

Food safety.

Public sanitation.

What I said and did strongly influenced the public's perception of the problem at hand. This was especially true where emergency response was concerned. Hence, I found myself constantly walking the thin line between scaring the hell out of the public and encouraging them to take action about a particular issue. More often than not, I felt that tightrope walkers had an easier time than I did.

When I sat down to write this book about the millennium bug, I decided to apply the same practical and level-headed approach I used at the Health Department. My intent is not to frighten you but, rather, to inform you so that you can make the best decision for yourself and your loved ones where Y2K is concerned. Fear, although a good motivator at times, can paralyze and prevent action from being taken. *And action, in this particular instance, is exactly what is required.*

My research on the implications of Y2K on our society was quite disturbing. When I started hunting for information, I deliberately turned my back on sensational tabloid articles, doomsday-hyped Web sites, and public paranoia. Instead, I focused on official government agency assessments and interviews with people who had inside knowledge of what was being done . . . or, conversely, not being done. My investigative efforts took me to the Department of Energy, Small Business Administration, Federal Aviation Administration, Department of Defense, U.S. Congress, American Red Cross, Federal Emergency Management Agency, Securities and Exchange Commission, Food and Drug Administration, Department of Agriculture, Federal Reserve Board, National Credit Union Administration, Department of Treasury, Nuclear Regulatory Commission, the Congressional Subcommittee on Government Management, Information and Technology, Social Security Administration, Federal Deposit Insurance Corporation, Federal Finance Institutions Examination Council, Senate Special Committee on the Year 2000 Technology Problem, Nuclear Energy Institute, General Accounting Office, Environmental Protection Agency, Department of Commerce, Department of Transportation, General Services Administration, Federal Trade Commission, Department of Health and

Human Services, President's Council on the Year 2000 Conversion, and the newly formed Critical Infrastructure Assurance Office. I also browsed through the archives of two respected news-wire organizations, the Associated Press and Reuters. From my personal experience with news organizations over the years, I consider these two print services to be the best at collecting information and accurately presenting the news to the public.

Initially, I felt certain that my research would alleviate any reservations I had about the possible ugly consequences of Y2K. But I was wrong. Terribly wrong. After I had read through some 450 documents, what I have learned only distresses me even more than before I started this book.

The millennium bug is, *without a doubt*, going to affect you, your communities and businesses, and the way in which you live. Our nation's entire infrastructure is at stake. Exactly how much disruption there will be come January 1, 2000, remains to be seen, but numerous year 2000 "bug bites" are already being reported around the world. At the beginning of 1999 for instance, 11 states were unable to make unemployment payments because of a Y2K computer glitch; their computers could not read 00 as a real date. As a result, some of these states had to resort to writing benefit checks by hand until the computers were fixed. For the recipients who depended on these checks to pay their bills and buy food, it was a shocking and anxious experience.

This is only the beginning.

Indeed, it is the match that precedes the conflagration.

You will learn about other computer malfunctions that have already happened as you read through the remainder of this book.

Which brings me to an important issue: *you.* You obviously feel uncomfortable about the future and what it holds, otherwise you would not be holding this book and reading these words.

As you will quickly realize, I deliberately wrote and organized this book to meet your needs. For instance, I encapsulated information into 101 practical tips. Although the length of each entry varies with the amount of information presented, each is a solid nugget of advice that warrants your attention.

Some of the tips may initially sound absurd to you. For instance, why should you collect items for bartering purposes? Or why should you pay off your debt? The reason for these—and other—suggestions is because no one truly knows how bad Y2K is going to make things in 1999 and 2000. Hence, we have to anticipate and prepare for the worst-case scenarios. And that includes stockpiling items for bartering purposes, such as handtools so that people can make repairs to generators, car engines, and camp stoves. It also means reducing your present debt since you may lose your job as a result of Y2K's handiwork; your creditors will expect their monthly payment regardless of your employment status.

Second, each chapter addresses a single topic that you need to focus your full attention on, such as food, water, or finance. By taking this approach, you absorb information in brain-digestible chunks—topic by topic—without becoming overwhelmed. It also allows you to quickly find information later on when you need it, without having to squint and scroll through an index of itty-bitty print.

And last, topic-related resources are listed near the end of each chapter in a box labeled "Check It Out . . . Yourself." I know that many people like to verify for themselves information they are reading. That's fine, and I encourage you to do so. Every "Check It Out . . ." directs you to several Internet Web sites you can visit and search through for additional information. If, however, you are hunting for topical listings, such as food-supply vendors, you will find those in one of the Appendices.

I will be the first to admit that the act of preparing for the unexpected can be an intimidating, emotional, and overwhelming process. However, by following the guidance outlined in this book, you and your loved ones will overcome these obstacles and be able to confidently confront the technological storm that has gathered on the horizon. You will be able to welcome the new millennium with open arms.

Prudence . . . not panic!

—Stephen Tomajczyk
March 5, 1999

the Y2K Crisis

The Bite of the Millennium Bug

A TECHNOLOGICAL STORM GATHERS ON THE HORIZON

It can only be attributed to human error.
—HAL-9000 computer, *2001: A Space Odyssey*

Arthur C. Clarke, author of the classic 1968 movie *2001: A Space Odyssey*, was more prophetic than he ever realized. In the movie, the sentient HAL-9000 computer aboard the spaceship USS *Discovery* goes haywire, forcing the astronauts to scramble and disconnect it. It was a prime example of technology going sour and of man giving computers too much control. In many regards, *2001* foreshadowed the Y2K problem that we are confronted with today.

TIP 1 *Educate yourself about Y2K.*

The so-called "millennium bug" was born decades ago when computers were the size of entire rooms and used reels of magnetic tape and stacks of punch cards to run a program. Since computer memory was extremely limited at that time (e.g., 64k), programmers decided to conserve memory by condensing the space used for dates. They accomplished this by eliminating the century designation 19 from the year. Hence, 1961 was abbreviated to 61. The 19 was assumed. This meant that a date like Valentine's Day, February 14, 1977, became 02/14/77.

Since then, this space-saving shortcut has been incorporated into thousands of software programs the world over. No one really gave it a second thought. Programmers automatically allocated space for six digits whenever a software program needed a date reference. This practice quickly spilled over into written documents. For example, if you have ever filled out an application form of any kind, the request for your date of birth probably looked like this: DOB __/__/__ or this: DOB __-__-__.

These formats make it easier for someone to enter the numbers into a computer database. Three spaces for six numbers: month, day, and year.

Now, my grandmother once said that the problem about shortcuts is, more often than not, they aren't. You generally end up with more work and problems than if you had done it the long way. Y2K only reaffirms her observation. Come January 1, 2000, any software program or computer chip that is date sensitive, measures time differences, etc. will translate that date as being 01-01-00. Or, to be more precise, January 1, 1900. Hence, the computer will be 100 years off the actual date. This applies to any date in the 21st century: computers will assume that 11/28/52 is November 28, 1952, instead of November 28, 2052, and that 04/11/01 is April 11, 1901, instead of April 11, 2001.

This poses a tremendous problem. With the arrival of the year 2000, some computers may "crash" and stop working, or they may get confused about what day it is and spew out incorrect information. In fact, any computer calculation that involves a date—such as benefit checks, insurance, or interest payments—will very likely be wrong.

Unlike generations before us, we rely heavily on digital technology—from ATMs to gasoline pumps, and from pagers to fax machines. Small wonder that people are worried about the possible consequences of computers going bonkers on New Year's, 2000. This is especially true since many of our systems are linked to several others. If one component crashes, it could topple all the others in the same system, much like one domino knocking over another. Examples of integrated computer systems include banking services, utilities, and national defense. This is why Y2K is sometimes referred to by doomsayers as the "millennium meltdown."

THE TRUMPET IS SOUNDED

The Y2K crisis is not new. Programmers, as long as 40 years ago, realized that eventually there was going to be a problem when December 31, 1999, showed up on the calendars. But they were optimists: they were confident that programmers who came after them would work with more advanced and powerful computer systems that would not be restricted to six-digit dates. These computers, for instance, would be able to tell the difference between 1976 and 2076. Thus, there would be no Y2K crisis.

Unfortunately, the programmers and information technology professionals were overly optimistic. Although computers have indeed increased in speed and memory capability, the archaic six-digit date system is still widely used today.

July 1996 proved to be the turning point for the millennium bug. That's when Senator Daniel P. Moynihan (D-NY) sent the following letter to the White House alerting President Clinton about the problem and its possible consequences:

Dear Mr. President:

I hope this letter reaches you. I write to alert you to a problem, which could have extreme negative economic consequences during your second term. The "Year 2000 Time Bomb." This has to do with the transition of computer programs from the 20th to the 21st century.

The main computer languages from the '50s and '60s, such as COBOL, FORTRAN and Assembler, were designed to minimize consumption of computer memory by employing date fields providing for only six digits. The date of this letter in "computerese," for example, is 96-07-31. The century designation "19" is assumed.

The problem is that many programs will read January 1, 2000, as January 1, 1900. Computer programs do not recognize the 21st century without a massive rewriting of computer code.

I first learned of all this in February and requested a study by *the Congressional Research Service. The study, just now completed, substantiated the worst fears of the doomsayers. The Year 2000 Problem ("Y2K") is worldwide. Each line of computer code needs to be analyzed and either passed on or rewritten. The banking system is particularly vulnerable. A money center bank may have 500 million lines of code to be revised at a cost of $1 per line. That's a $500 million problem. One would expect that a quick fix of the problem would have been found, but it hasn't happened and the experts tell me it is not likely.*

There are three issues. First, the cost of reviewing and rewriting code for federal and state governments, which will range in the billions of dollars over the next three years. Second, the question of whether there is time enough to get the job done and, if not, what sort of triage we may need. I am particularly concerned about the IRS and Social Security in this respect. Third, the question of what happens to the economy if the problem is not resolved by mid-1999. Are corporations and consumers not likely to withhold spending decisions and possibly even withdraw funds from banks if they fear the economy is facing chaos?

I have a recommendation. A presidential aide should be appointed to take responsibility for assuring that all federal agencies, including the military, be Y2K date compliant by January 1, 1999, and that all commercial and industrial firms doing business with the federal government also be compliant by that date. I am advised that the Pentagon is further ahead on the curve here than any of the federal agencies. You may wish to turn to the military to take command of dealing with the problem.

The computer has been a blessing; if we don't act quickly, however, it could become the curse of the age.

Respectfully,
Daniel Patrick Moynihan

It took the White House more than a year after receiving Moynihan's letter to make its first public acknowledgment of the millennium bug. At a press conference on August 15, 1997, President Clinton stated that Americans need not worry about the "computer clock" problem. Several months later, however, in February 1998, John Koskinen was appointed by Clinton as the federal Y2K czar. This move finally demonstrated that the White House was taking the millennium bug seriously. But, as you will learn, the action was too little, too late.

EXTERMINATING THE BUG

It doesn't take a rocket scientist to figure out how to squash the millennium bug. Essentially, it requires that every com-

---

GOVERNMENT REPORT CARD

E ach quarter, Congressman Stephen Horn (R-CA) hands out a report card that shows how well the government is preparing for Y2K. As the chairman of the House Subcommittee on Government Management, Information and Technology, Horn is well briefed on progress being made on the millennium bug.

To date, the effort has been abysmal. The latest report card— February 1999—gave the government a C+ for its overall efforts. That's up from a D in December 1998. Although this appears to be promising, it is not. The six agencies that prevented the government from earning a higher grade—the departments of Agriculture, Defense, Health and Human Services, State, and Transportation—have more than 50 percent of the mission-critical computer systems in the federal government. In other words, if these agencies are not ready for Y2K by December 31, 1999, then half the government's computers could crash.

Ironically, even receiving an A is no guarantee that a department is 100 percent Y2K compliant. In fact, of the 11 departments and agencies that received an A:

- Only one has finished embedded-systems repairs.
- Four still have not completed repairs or testing on data exchanges.
- Eight have not completed repairs on telecommunications equipment.
- Six have not completed contingency plans.

"Year 2000 Progress Report Card" on page 20 lists the good, the bad, and the ugly.

puter program be reviewed and corrected. In extreme cases, the entire computer system may need to be replaced. Sounds pretty simple, doesn't it? You just get all the big companies to repair their Y2K problems and then have them force their vendors and smaller suppliers to do the same thing or risk being dropped as a business partner.

The problem with this approach is that it represents an enormous undertaking. A Herculean effort, by the way, that our government and companies have seriously underestimated, both timewise and costwise.

You see, every single line of computer code has to be carefully scrutinized. For some programs, this can mean 5 million lines of code or more.

Making matters worse is the way dates are actually recorded within a computer program. For example, March 2, 1966—my sister's birthday—is usually abbreviated by most people as 3/2/66. But if you have European heritage, you would probably write it as 2/3/66. Other ways to write this birthdate include:

03/02/66
02/03/66
1966/03/02
1966/02/03
Mar/2/66

Thus, you cannot simply order the computer to add "19" to the last two digits of the date computer field to make it a complete year. Doing so, you may actually be adding "19" to the day of your birth, which, in this example, would be either "192" or "1902."

Complicating all this is the fact that many computer systems today are antiquated. When people hear the word "computer," it is safe to say that they think of desktop or laptop computers like Gateway, Macintosh, and IBM.

Old mainframes—those created 20 to 30 years ago—are still in use, most notably in state and federal government agencies. These antiquated "steel boxes" were originally programmed using now-bygone languages like COBOL, C, Assembler, and

FORTRAN. Few people today know these languages; the original programmers are either retired or deceased. And, adding insult to injury, records were not kept. So, no one really knows how to fix Y2K problems in mainframes. For those rare folks that do, they simply don't have time to get all the corrections made before January 1, 2000, arrives.

CHIPS 'N' DIP, ANYONE?

Even if a miracle occurs and every single computer in the world is suddenly cleansed of the millennium bug, failures, problems, and crises will still happen. This is because of the so-called "embedded chip."

The best way to describe what an embedded chip is and what it does is to have you imagine a large bowl of onion dip and a bag of potato chips.

Pretend that the onion dip is a system of some sort. A system is supposed to *do something*, such as turn on a light or operate a microwave oven. Now, take a potato chip from the bag, smash it into tiny pieces, pick up one crumb, and then plunge it deep into the onion dip. (You can mentally lick the dip off your finger if you'd like.) That's an embedded chip. It is the miniature computer brain that tells the dip exactly what to do, when to do it, and how to do it. Sometimes a system (the onion dip) needs just one chip to make it operate properly. Most complex systems, however, require hundreds or even thousands of chips. For example, an offshore oil rig has upward of 100 embedded systems, each containing as many as 10,000 individual chips.

According to the Gartner Group, a consulting firm, there are more than 25 *billion* embedded chips in America. They are literally found in everything, everywhere: fax machines, HVAC, voice mail systems, backup power systems, grocery store scanners, aircraft avionics, ATMs, gas station pumps, bank vaults, postage machines, microwave ovens, thermostats, automobiles, elevators, pagers, telephones, building security systems, medical devices (e.g., pacemakers, infusion pumps,

MRI, CT scan, heart monitors, dialysis, lab equipment), postal machines, flow meters, shipping services, prison security systems, electronic hotel keys, printing presses, and fire alarms. They are also found and used in manufacturing control systems, financial systems, utilities, the stock market, national defense, personal computers, and transportation.

A good portion of these embedded chips—no one really has a good number, although 50 million is sometimes mentioned—have date-related information programmed into them. Therein lies the crisis. Will these minicomputers celebrate New Year's Day 2000 a bit too heartily and crash? Experts say that many of them will indeed fail if they are not corrected. Problem is, they just don't know which ones will crash or when. The chips might simply stop working, or they may go wild and give unpredictable results.

Although engineers need only to test the system (the onion dip) to figure out whether it is Y2K compliant—and not each and every chip that is embedded in the system—it is still impossible for anyone to accomplish this by the end of 1999. To put it bluntly, there is no way every embedded system can be found and corrected.

Because of the sheer number of embedded chips in our society, failures are inevitable. Sporadic power failures will probably occur, along with failures in water and sewer systems, traffic controls, medical devices, fuel delivery systems, and telecommunication systems, to name a few. A special Senate report released in February 1999 acknowledges the possibilities of problems: ". . . We believe that disruptions will occur that in some cases will be significant."

Do *not* dismiss the seriousness represented by these so-called "chips in the dip." They could have life-threatening consequences.

For example, in an article that appeared in the *St. Louis Post-Dispatch*, Y2K expert Peter de Jaeger said that a manufacturer of volatile gas discovered faulty embedded chips in its system. When the date was moved forward to 2000, the chip failed and shut off a valve that, in turn, would have shut down the cooling system. A company executive admitted to de Jaeger that a cooling system shutdown would have caused an explosion. The company, needless to say, has since replaced the chips.

To give another example, as frequently told by Senator Robert F. Bennett (R-UT), a water-purification plant in Utah ran a Y2K preparedness test by setting the clocks ahead to January 1, 2000. The plant's embedded systems supposedly malfunctioned, dumping lethal amounts of chlorine and fluoride into the water. Although the plant has since corrected the problem, it plans, along with other water-treatment plants in Utah, to install and update backup power generators, just in case Y2K disrupts the regional power grid.

HOW MANY PROBLEMS?

In October 1998, the Gartner Group released a report titled "Year 2000 Global State of Readiness and Risks to the General Business Community." It details what percentage of companies in a given country will experience a major Y2K failure. The results are alarming, especially given the fact that the United States is attached to these nations by a digital umbilical cord. If things crash overseas, it very well could have a ripple effect here.

15% Failure	33% Failure	50% Failure	66% Failure
United States	France	Hong Kong	Russia
Canada	Italy	Japan	China
England	Singapore	Argentina	Romania
Norway	Mexico	Venezuala	Egypt
Denmark	Chile	Saudi Arabia	Thailand
Sweden	Finland	Germany	Pakistan
Switzerland	Brazil	India	Sudan
Australia	Spain	S. Africa	Morocco
Netherlands	Peru		
Israel			

THE RESPONSE: WALK, DON'T RUN

As should be evident to you by now, Y2K is a serious issue. It is a very simple computer glitch that has the power to disrupt our way of life. It is a modern-day David that is able to slay Goliath with a single keystroke or mouse click. It is a technological Pearl Harbor.

Unfortunately, the United States and the rest of the world took a nonchalant "walk, don't run" approach to Y2K. We simply did not anticipate the extent of the problem (i.e., embedded chips), the amount of time that it would take to examine and fix a system (one programmer told me that it took nine months just to make one bank Y2K compliant), and how expensive the repairs would be. With regard to the latter, the consultant group Cap Gemini America projects that fixing the Y2K problem is going to cost America $655 billion. That's more than the entire cost of the Vietnam War, which totaled $500 billion. The cost to fix the problem worldwide is presently estimated to be $1.4 trillion.

To put it bluntly, we started far too late with too few resources. Now we are frantically trying to play catch-up, but it is a losing battle, as illustrated by the following news reports:

- The U.S. Army admits that it will miss the Office of Management and Budget's Year 2000 deadline for having all its systems ready. (January 26, 1999)
- In a survey done by Cap Gemini, 92 percent of organizations report that they have missed crucial Y2K deadlines. (January 11, 1999)
- AT&T admits that it will not be ready for Y2K. (January 4, 1999, Source: Michael Hyatt)
- Chevron Corp. says that its systems may be vulnerable to significant failures as they try to deal with the Y2K problem. (January 4, 1999)
- According to SEC filings, not one publicly held electric company is year 2000 ready. (December 28, 1998)
- According to the National Association of Counties, one-third of counties in America are not even aware of the

millennium bug, and only half have a plan in place to deal with potential failures in the year 2000. (December 22, 1998)

- Nearly 90 percent of American companies are two to four months behind in their Y2K repair project target dates. (December 15, 1998)
- GM must upgrade or replace 7,600 business computer systems. The auto manufacturer must also examine and possibly replace 1.7 million computer devices that control everything from lighting systems to robotic welding equipment. (December 8, 1998, Source: Michael Hyatt)

The Federal Emergency Management Agency (FEMA) has begun meeting with state-level emergency management people to identify critical issues and discuss contingency plans. In other words, FEMA has turned its eye away from Y2K prevention efforts and has begun focusing on postdisaster survival and cleanup. They realize that many companies and government agencies—who are literally months and years behind in eliminating Y2K problems—have now adopted a "fix on failure" approach. They are waiting for crises to strike first, before responding.

"Potential problems need to be identified and addressed now," FEMA deputy director Mike Walker told the media. "While some failures will be minor annoyances, some may have more serious consequence."

FEMA officials began their multistate tour at the end of January 1999.

Meanwhile, America's so-called Y2K czar, John A. Koskinen, has ordered that all existing emergency response centers operated by the Pentagon, U.S. intelligence agencies, and FEMA be merged together in some fashion so that millennium bug problems can be addressed in a united manner. Canada has already taken this step. In fact, Canada plans to initiate martial law because of Y2K. (This shocking news was acknowledged by Senator Bob Bennett in a recent *World Net Daily* article.)

At the state level, several states have alerted their National Guard units to prepare for possible riots, bank runs, and looting that may result from Y2K. Kentucky, for example, plans to activate 300 troops. Ohio is creating a mobilization plan in case the governor declares a state of emergency. In Washington, the National Guard is getting ready to mobilize half its troops. In Wisconsin, legislation was recently passed to mobilize the National Guard to respond to Y2K emergencies. And, as for Maryland and other states, they are still discussing the issue, with final decisions to be made by summer 1999.

If the National Guard is indeed deployed, the troops will not only be used for security matters—as described above— but they will also be used to provide emergency shelter and medical services, transportation, water distribution, cleanup services, search and rescue operations, and portable generators.

TIP 2 **Understand what crises could arise.**

As you read about Y2K in magazines and books and on Internet Web sites, you will see the word *teotwawki* from time to time. Is it a foreign phrase of some sort? Nope (although it *does* sound like a dish on an Indian restaurant menu). Actually, *teotwawki* is an acronym for The End Of The World As We Know It. It is increasingly being used in reference to Y2K because the bug has the power to turn our society upside down if the worst-case scenarios occur.

Now that you know how Y2K came about and how difficult it is to fix it, let's explore what crises are likely to arise as a result of it. This, in turn, will allow you to figure out how to best prepare yourself and your family for various situations.

First, you need to know that there are four ways the millennium bug can do damage. Understanding this will enable you to later understand the more catastrophic events that could happen.

The first kind of damage is known as *direct damage*. Direct

MILLENNIUM BUG HOTLINE

Feeling nervous about the millennium bug? Well, now you can call a toll-free hotline (888-USA-4-Y2K) for the latest information about the impending computer crisis. The hotline, which is operated by President Clinton's Council on the Year 2000 Conversion, offers information provided by government agencies, companies, and industry groups on a variety of topics, including banking, telecommunications, and household products. The topics are prerecorded and are available 24 hours a day. If, however, you wish to speak with a person, information specialists are available 9:00 A.M. to 8:00 P.M. EST, Monday through Friday.

damage is what most people think of first: what millennium bug problems are going to directly "bite" us? This typically involves digital products that we rely on, such as a PC or fax machine. If it ceases to function or, worse, it continues to operate but provides incorrect information, we could be in financial ruin.

Indirect damage is similar, but it refers to problems that happen to other entities—vendors, regulators, customers— that may eventually affect you. A good example of this would be if the company you work for is unable to give you a paycheck because there is a Y2K problem with your company's bank or payroll processing firm.

Ambient damage is a general disruption caused by the millennium bug. For example, an electric company could be swamped with thousands of calls from worried citizens who want to know if the utility's computers have crashed. Obviously, an incident like this would disrupt the utility's normal operations and prevent real calls about local power outages from getting through. Another, often quoted, example of ambient damage would be a run on the banking system, with people anxiously withdrawing money from their accounts. Again, this would disrupt normal operations and, more important, it would stress the financial reserve system.

The last type of damage is *causal damage*. In this case, the

Y2K problems are embedded in products that a company has made and distributed to others. This generally involves hardware or software products (which you could buy or receive free of charge through a direct mail promotion), but it could also involve items that have embedded chips, such as pagers and medical devices.

The big question among computer experts, government officials, and Y2K doomsayers is this: How much damage will the millennium bug do? Will it cause just one kind of damage, several types of damage, or all four types of damage? And will the damage happen all at once—say on January 1, 2000—or over a period of time?

In general, experts admit that Y2K failures are inevitable. They point to Y2K compliance as being the culprit. Exactly how, they wonder, will computer systems that are certified as being Y2K compliant work when they encounter a noncompliant system—say, for example, a brokerage house's computer with the New York Stock Exchange? Will they fight and crash?

For that matter, how will two compliant systems interact with each other? After all, there is no universal standard with regard to the definition of *compliant*. What the Pentagon declares as being Y2K compliant may not meet the definition that Boeing or General Dynamics uses. Hence, there could still be battles fought between computers that have allegedly been "fixed."

ARMAGEDDON?

If it runs its *absolute worst course*, the millennium bug has the power to transport our nation back 150 years to the 1850s, much like the tornado did to Dorothy by sending her and Toto to the land of Oz. There are four apocalyptic scenarios that could achieve this level of societal disintegration: power outages, distribution problems, financial meltdown, and war.

National Blackout

Of all the things that could fail, electricity is the worst thing we could lose to Y2K. That's because electricity is tightly woven through every fabric of our society: ovens, refrigerators, traffic lights, the 911 system, hospital equipment, water purification systems, garage door openers, waste treatment plants, security systems, heating systems, lights, credit card systems, telephones, gas stations, computers, ATMs, water pumps, appliances . . . the list goes on.

Without electricity, America's businesses and manufacturing plants will shut down. That means no oil is produced or refined, no food is processed or packaged, and no water is pumped or distributed. Our nation is immediately cast into a dark and cold world.

Within days of the blackout, disease outbreaks will abruptly appear across America, involving millions of people. This will be due to people eating bacteria-laden foods that have been unrefrigerated or undercooked. It will also be attributed to people drinking contaminated water. Thanks to the unrefrigerated food rotting in thousands of warehouses, silos, homes, and restaurants, the insect and rodent populations will also explode. This will contribute to the spread of communicable diseases like plague and rat bite fever.

Although these ailing individuals will feel terrible, those who require advanced life support or a complex emergency operation—such as heart surgery—will very likely die. That's because hospitals without generators will simply be huge concrete shells housing worthless medical equipment that runs on electricity.

Similarly, crime will skyrocket as desperate people resort to desperate means to get the food, water, and shelter they need to survive. The poor and violent will prey on the rich and weak; blood will be spilled.

The longer the national blackout lasts, the worse things will become. Presently, experts say that most companies across America will go bankrupt if they lose power for more than seven days. There is simply no way they can recover their losses and get up and running again. So, if the power is off for two or three months, you won't have a job and you will probably be broke, having drained your bank accounts. Bartering and crime will be the two thriving industries then.

In the end, you will be living day to day, minute by minute. You will be struggling to find food and water, and trying desperately to stay warm. (Remember, January 1, 2000, is in the middle of winter!) You will also find yourself becoming intolerant of other people and being more willing to use violence to stay alive. The modern, high-tech world that you are so acquainted with today will wither away in a matter of days after the blackout occurs. In its place a new societal structure will arise—a fight-or-flight survival environment. Only the self-reliant, self-sufficient, and brutal will be able to endure.

Distribution Chaos

Stores and businesses maintain only a few days' or, in some industries, a few weeks' worth of inventory at any given time. Your local supermarket, for instance, generally has a two- or three-day supply of major food items.

Were Y2K to somehow cause America's distribution system to fail, we would notice it within a week's time. Gas stations would run dry. Supermarkets and convenience stores would be empty and closed. Restaurants and fast-food chains would be closed. Hospitals would run out of supplies. Malls would be empty. Mail would be undelivered. Drug prescriptions would be left unfilled. Manufacturers would have production slowdowns, followed quickly by layoffs.

In the end, America's industrial sector would collapse. Companies simply cannot survive if they are unable to distribute and sell their goods. And, in a catch-22 fashion, people cannot buy goods if they do not have a job that gives them a paycheck. Hence, the entire economy disintegrates.

This means you and your family will eventually run out of food, gas, heating oil, general supplies, etc. A black market will arise and you will undoubtedly find yourself trading or bartering for the goods you need. You will also find yourself learning how to sew clothes and repair appliances and engines since retail stores will be empty. It also means that you'll be doing a lot of walking, since your car will be useless without any gasoline.

Financial Meltdown

People's fear of losing money is what could rocket the world into another Great Depression. If a bank has a Y2K malfunction, for instance, it will experience a bank run—as will other banks in the area once the incident becomes public knowledge. With people standing 150 deep in line to withdraw their money, a tremendous stress will be placed on the bank itself, since it usually only has 2 percent of its deposits in the vault. This means the bank will have to either temporarily shut its doors or limit withdrawals to reasonable amounts, say $100 per week per person. (Remember the movie *It's a Wonderful Life*?)

Either option will only serve to fan the flames of public fear. Those of you who endured the great savings-and-loan scandals in the 1980s know exactly what this is like. Within a few days, bank runs will be a regional phenomenon, then a national one. This, in turn, will panic stock market investors around the world. Now what once was a single bank problem has rapidly expanded into a global crisis.

In a similar fashion, if public confidence wanes over companies being able to meet Y2K compliance in time for New Year's Day 2000, investors will begin withdrawing their money from the stock market by fall 1999. Why? Because it makes absolutely no sense to invest in companies or mutual funds that might go belly-up because of a computer glitch.

Regardless of which of these two scenario pans out, the results are identical. First, the world economy will collapse, causing a severe recession or depression. Second, you won't have money on hand to buy food and supplies or to pay your bills.

At the time of this writing—February 1999—many economists are publicly warning of a recession by year's end. Ed Yardeni of Deutsche Bank in New York is predicting a 70 percent chance of a major recession.

Similarly, John Westergaard, publisher of Westergaard On-line Systems, testified before the U.S. Senate Special Committee on the Year 2000 Technology Problem that there will be a worldwide Y2K recession.

"The question isn't 'Will there be a recession?'" he informed the committee. "It is, 'How bad will it be?'"

War

As most people in the free world would agree, Iraq's Saddam Hussein is a coward and an opportunist. During the 1990s, Hussein routinely left the safety of his underground air raid bunker to thumb his nose at the United States, even though he was surrounded by smoking craters. He lied, cheated, and deceived whenever it benefited him. If he thought he could get away with something, such as poisoning Kurds with poison gas, he did it.

It is this sense of opportunism that could trigger a war. If

CHECK IT OUT . . . YOURSELF

Does your state have a Y2K plan in place?
   www.nasire.org/ss/ST2000.html
   www.y2k.com/non-us-fedgov.htm

State Y2K Web site listings
   www.dir.state.tx.us/y2k/resources/index.htm

Are the electric utilities ready?
   www.euy2k.com

U.S. government progress report card
   www.house.gov/reform/gmit

Year 2000 updates
   www.y2knews.com
   www.y2ktimebomb.com
   www.y2ktoday.com
   www.year2000.com
   www.msnbc.com/news/227213.asp

Saddam Hussein believes that America's armed forces—with all their high-tech weapons and gadgetry—will be rendered impotent as a result of the millennium bug on January 1, 2000, it is quite possible that he would order his troops south into Kuwait and Saudi Arabia to take control of the world's oil supply. Needless to say, if he did do this, no democratic nation on earth would allow it to happen without mounting a large-scale military response to thwart it. Hence, a regional war could ensue.

Business analyst Richard Maybury, who specializes in geo-politics and economics, has been predicting a war like this since early 1998. "The evidence indicates that the world has entered another period of major upheaval," he wrote in his annual forecast. He goes on to state that the war could be on the scale of World War I and that it will be fought in two theaters: Europe and the Middle East.

What is frightening about this prediction is that Maybury has a long history of accurately predicting crises. For example, he predicted the October 1987 stock market crash . . . five months before it happened. He also predicted the collapse of the Soviet Union . . . two years in advance. And he predicted the 1991 Gulf War . . . a year ahead.

If a war does indeed erupt, it will adversely affect the stock markets, your job, your income, and your way of life. You can expect to ration supplies and to live on much less than what you earn now.

A CALL TO ACTION

Do these scenarios frighten or depress you? They should. They do, after all, represent the *extreme* of what could occur: teot-wawki. I am not suggesting that any of these crises will happen. *In fact, I fully expect the world to be here come January 1, 2000, and beyond.* But, on the other hand, I don't expect the world to be a bright, rosy place. I personally am anticipating sporadic power outages and a severe recession.

The reason these apocalyptic examples are presented is to

YEAR 2000 PROGRESS REPORT CARD

	98 May 15	98 Aug 15	98 Nov 13	99 Feb 12	2000 Final
SSA Social Security Administration	A+	A	A	A	
NRC Nuclear Regulatory Commission	B	D	C−	A	
NSF National Science Foundation	A−	A	A	A	
SBA Small Business Administration	B	A	A	A	
EPA Environmental Protection Agency	F	B	B+	A	
HUD Dept of Housing and Urban Development	C	C	C	A−	
VA Department of Veterans Affairs	C	B−	B−	A−	
GSA General Services Administration	A−	B+	B+	A−	
Interior Department of the Interior	C−	D	B	A−	
Education Department of Education	D	F	C−	A−	
OPM Office of Personnel Management	C−	D	C−	A−	
FEMA Federal Emergency Management Agency	A−	B−	B	B+	
NASA National Aeronautics and Space Admin	B	C+	C+	B+	
Commerce Department of Commerce	B	B	B	B	
Justice Department of Justice	D	F	F	B	

	98 May 15	98 Aug 15	98 Nov 13	99 Feb 12	2000 Final
Labor Department of Labor	C	D	C	B	
DOE Department of Energy	F	F	F	B	
Treasury Department of the Treasury	C	D+	C	B –	
HHS Dept of Health and Human Services	F	F	F	C+	
Agriculture Department of Agriculture	D	C	C	C	
DOD Department of Defense	D	D	D –	C –	
State Department of State	F	F	F	F	
DOT Department of Transportation	F	D	D	F	
AID Agency for International Development	F	F	F	F	
Administration Overall Federal Departments and Agencies	F	D	D	C+	

www.house.gov/reform/gmit

Prepared for Subcommittee Chairman Stephen Horn. Subcommittee on Government Management, Information and Technology. Issued February 22, 1999, based on agency data from February 12, 1999. Subcommittee Home Page on the Internet: http://www.house.gov/refom/gmit

give you an idea of what you need to prepare for. There is a common thread through all these calamities: the need for readily available cash, water, food, and basic supplies. The remainder of this book will help you decide what things you should stockpile, and in what quantities. It will also help you better understand what steps you should take to protect your assets, such as money, valuables, and investments. And the book will provide insight on how a crisis—regardless of size—could emotionally and mentally influence your life.

Prepare! Don't Despair

Y2 CARE ABOUT Y2K . . . B4 IT'S 2L8

> The greatest antidote to worry, whether you're getting
> ready for a space flight or facing a problem of daily life,
> is preparation. The more you prepare, the more you study, the
> more you think, the more you try to envision what might
> happen and what your best response and options are, the more
> you are able to allay your fears about the future. . . .
> —Senator John H. Glenn, Jr. (D-OH)
> *Parade*, October 25, 1998

Being prepared does *not* mean you are paranoid. It simply means that you want to protect yourself, your family, and your home from harm. It is an admirable and innate trait that is at the heart of self-preservation.

Being prepared has absolutely nothing to do with paranoia, but it has *everything* to do with prudence. My grandparents taught me this lesson, which was reinforced by years of scouting (I was an Eagle Scout) and, later on, by my involvement in Public Health emergencies. My grandparents lived through the Great Depression of 1929–39, and they never forgot it. Even some 50 years after the Depression ended, when I visited them in Michigan, I could still find little stockpiles of supplies scattered throughout their house: loose change hidden under bath towels, extra soap and shampoo stacked in closets, surplus food kept in a second refrigerator, and canned goods stashed away in the basement. They knew what it was like to endure a severe hardship and they never wanted to be caught off guard again.

Floods, fires, hurricanes, and tornadoes aside, America has not experienced a major nationwide disaster in some 70 years. And it has *never* been confronted with the prospect of a global technological failure. The millennium bug is a new threat. It is an imposing threat that leaves many of us feeling frightened,

confused, and anxious. We have no idea what the consequences of Y2K will be or how severe an impact it will have on
our lives.

Likewise, many of us—softened by technology's comfort—do not know how to prepare for such an unknown
threat. Yet, deep down inside, many of us sense that we should
be doing something now—today, in fact—to minimize Y2K's
impact on ourselves and our loved ones. That is what this book
is all about. And it starts right here. . . .

TIP ③ ***Do not panic. Overcome your anxiety and begin preparing today.***

If you allow yourself to reflect on the Y2K crisis for
any length of time, it is easy to find yourself exploring some
fairly horrifying scenarios. This is especially true if you have a
creative imagination. Power failures, nuclear meltdowns, unemployment, riots, and food shortages are dreadful enough
possibilities to cause anyone to hyperventilate, panic, and toss
and turn all night long.

If this describes your feelings, then let me reassure you: it is
perfectly okay to feel anxious and overwhelmed about Y2K.
Feeling this way is a natural response. In fact, it is Mother
Nature's way of letting you know that you are in a tenuous,
and possibly dangerous, situation and you need to be on
guard. So don't feel bad or guilty about your anxieties. I'll be
the first to admit that I have had my fair share of trepidation
and sleepless nights where Y2K is concerned.

The goal here, though, is not to allow your fear to paralyze
you and prevent you from doing what you need to do to minimize Y2K's impact on your life.

How do you do that? Think about the positive things that
will come about if you make preparations. For instance, if Y2K
proves to be all hype, then you will still be prepared for any
natural disaster that may strike.

Kim, who lives in North Carolina, has taken this upbeat
approach to dealing with her Y2K preparations.

PEOPLE ARE PREPARING

A January 1999 poll done by the *Journal Sentinel* reveals that Americans nationwide are beginning to prepare for possible Y2K failures. Of the respondents who had heard about the Y2K crisis, 77 percent said they were concerned about it. So what are they doing to prepare? Several things, including: stockpiling food and water (24 percent), setting aside cash for emergencies (21 percent), buying a generator (20 percent), stockpiling fuels (11 percent), purchasing an alternative heating source (10 percent), selling their stocks or mutual funds (6 percent), and buying a firearm (5 percent).

Similarly, those who work in the computer industry are worried about Y2K as well. In an Internet poll of 6,300 information technology professionals, nearly 80 percent of those surveyed admitted that they are taking steps to minimize the impact of Y2K. How? Well, 62 percent plan to avoid traveling, 61 percent will withdraw money from the bank, and 58 percent will buy extra food and supplies in case of a shortage.

This is an important group of people to listen to since they are the ones who are responsible for fixing the Y2K problem. If they are concerned enough to be taking precautions, so should you.

I feel I should be ready (for Y2K), just in case. If everything goes well, then the food I've collected can be eaten slowly or given to the needy. The more I have thought about things, the more I have come to understand how necessary it really is to have a short supply of goods on hand. Things could go haywire at any moment for several reasons, and we would not be prepared. We depend too much on outside sources for everything, and I think from now on I will keep some stuff on hand, like I do now, for a possible catastrophe.

See? Kim has replaced her fear with a common-sense approach to emergency preparedness. She is not panicking. Wisely, Kim sees herself deliberately and methodically preparing for any future disaster, whether it is Y2K or a hurricane. She clearly sees the benefits of her actions: if nothing happens, then the food can be eaten by her family or given away to the poor. (She has overlooked one thing, though: depending on who she donates the food to, it could be tax deductible. If it is, that's icing on the cake!)

In her E-mail, Kim went on to share her personal experiences of dealing with natural disasters, including a blizzard that left her family trapped in a trailer without water or electricity for a week. I list sections of it here to give you an idea of what life without basic amenities is like:

Our saving grace was the gas stove that we used for heat. Josh was a baby and we had to bring his crib into the small kitchen along with our mattress. We blocked off the rest of the house with blankets so we could survive in the kitchen. Bill (her husband) and I took turns turning the oven off and on during the night. I still froze. We had to melt snow to drink and wash the dishes. Bathing was out of the question. It was mightily cold going to the bathroom on an ice toilet. . . . I plan on doing everything in my power to be a little more comfortable in the event this occurs again for whatever reason.

If you are unable to eliminate your anxiety about preparing for Y2K, then tap your fear and use it to spur you to action.

Fear, when controlled, is a powerful motivator. Here are a few things you can focus on to propel you to action:

Y2K problems are already happening. In the United States alone, the Gartner Group anticipates that 15 percent of all businesses will suffer at least one major Y2K failure. Since there are 30,000 midsize companies and 6 million small businesses in the United States, that means some 905,000 companies will be affected.

Supplies are beginning to run low. Nearly every mail-order company that sells survival items and emergency food supplies is overwhelmed. For instance, orders for food supplies at some companies are back ordered six months. So the longer you wait to prepare, the less likely you will be able to purchase the items you want, whether bought at a local discount store or from a mail-order company.

Zero action gets you nothing. This is a very simple formula. If you do absolutely nothing to prepare, then you will have absolutely nothing if a Y2K failure or natural disaster happens. No groceries. No money. No water. No supplies. You may be able to live on nothing, but most children, pets, and family members cannot. Think of them and decide if they really should go without.

▶ TIP ◢ **4** *Do not do too much at once.*

When you prepare for Y2K, it is easy to go in a thousand different directions at once. A word of advice: don't. Doing so will only make you feel overwhelmed and depressed. You have more than enough things to do on a daily basis with work and family than to try adding another 30 or 40 balls to your juggling act.

Instead, be very focused in your preparedness efforts. Be logical and methodical. Do the self-assessment found in Chapter 3 and prioritize what you need to do. Then deliberately pursue them one at a time, at a pace that feels comfortable to you (acknowledging, of course, that you don't have five years to prepare).

Following this course of action will not only leave your household prepared but will significantly lessen your anxiety. You won't have a cloud of gloom and doom hanging over your head. You will have peace of mind that everything is done and ready.

▶ TIP **5** *Talk to your spouse and family about Y2K to gain their support.*

If you live alone then you can skip this section. You have no one to answer to but yourself as to what you do with your time and money. However, if you have a family, preparing for the millennium bug requires the support of your

BUG BITES

The millennium bug has been snacking on the world for many years now. We simply do not hear about these incidents because many of them are internal to a company, and the firm's management quietly sweep them under the mat. Here are several examples of the bug's eating binge:

- In Winona, MN, 104-year-old Mary Bandar received a letter telling her to register for kindergarten. Computers thought she was four years old.
- In Washington, D.C., a Department of Defense supplier with a contract for delivery of goods in 2003 received a warning that it was 94 years behind schedule.
- Godiva Chocolatier's retail stores were not able to handle credit cards with an expiration date later than 1999. Employees were told to manually enter the credit card information and to use a 12/99 expiration date to "trick" the computer into approving the purchase.
- Hundreds of records were deleted from the Unum Life Insurance Company's database after a computer mistook 00 in the date field to mean 1900 instead of 2000.
- In January 1998, AP tax writer Rob Wells reported that IRS computers informed about 1,000 taxpayers who were up-to-date in their tax installment payments that they were now, suddenly, in default. The problem, which was corrected, was caused by a Y2K programming error.
- When the U.S. Strategic Command—the unified military command that oversees America's nuclear forces—ran a Y2K test of its classified Internet Web page, the computer system crashed. The problem? Ironically, it was a graphic clock on the Web site that counted down the time remaining before the arrival of 2000.
- Computers at Amway Corporation rejected several batches of chemicals that the company uses to manufacture products because their expiration date seemed to be 100 years old—1900 instead of 2000.
- A computer glitch at Smith Barney accidentally put about $19 million into each of the firm's 525,000 financial management accounts. The error was quickly discovered and the money returned—much to the dismay of the suddenly mega-rich clients.

- *Money Magazine* reported that a computer network used to schedule patient appointments at three hospitals and 75 clinics in Pennsylvania suddenly shut down. The cause? Someone had entered an appointment for January 2000.
- At the 511-bed Hospital of St. Raphael in New Haven, CT, medical staff discovered 18 ventilators that were not Y2K compliant.
- In Orange County, NC, animal control officers became alarmed when computers showed a dramatic decrease in the number of rabies-vaccinated pets. It turned out that the county's computer was recording newly vaccinated cats and dogs as having received their shots in 1897 and, therefore, the shots' effectiveness had expired.

spouse and children. If you are unable to get them to understand the Y2K problem, you will be labeled as "crazy." Everyone will fight you tooth and nail as you try to redirect family time and money on preparedness issues. Without their support, you will be fighting a losing battle and gaining a lot of gray hair in the process.

My biggest obstacle to preparing is that my partner doesn't get it at all and thinks I'm insane.

—E-mail posted on www.MrsSurvival.com

Here are some suggested guidelines to follow when discussing Y2K preparedness with your loved ones:

Talk with your spouse first. It is best to discuss Y2K preparedness with your spouse before raising the topic among your children. That way both of you can present a united front—the children will see that you are in agreement with each other on the issue. (See Chapter 3 for tips on how to talk with your children about the millennium bug.)

Be nonthreatening. Approach your spouse when he or she is not involved in something important and say something like, "Hon, I'd like your advice on something that has been bothering me a lot lately. Can we set aside some time this week to do that?" More often than not, this approach will immediately get your spouse's full attention. After all, how often do you ask for advice? If he or she asks what the subject is, be honest. Say that it is disaster preparedness. State that you are very concerned about protecting the family and minimizing any possible damage to the home. Nearly everyone understands this and is willing to discuss it.

Set aside a specific time and place to talk. Y2K is a serious issue and it deserves the right atmosphere for you to discuss it—without interruptions from the television and playful children. So arrange to hold the conversation in the living room or dining room. Anywhere, as long as it is in a quiet place where you can focus on the topic at hand.

Also, do not expect that you will have only one meeting on Y2K—anticipate several meetings. It takes time to thoroughly discuss the various preparedness options you have available to you. Some families I know have weekly meetings to review what has been accomplished and to establish goals for what needs to be done in the upcoming weeks.

Compile a briefing packet on Y2K. There's no sense in trying to play the role of Y2K expert—your spouse won't believe it (unless, of course, you happen to be a computer programmer). So let other experts speak on your behalf: assemble a file folder or notebook of legitimate articles that discuss the Y2K problem and its possible consequences. When you begin your conversation about preparedness, point to this file folder, and say, "Here is some reading material about the millennium bug that you can read if you have any questions. It's what changed my mind about the whole thing, and I think you'll find it to be the same for you, too." What do you put in the portfolio? Download some documents and news reports from the Internet, including the federal government's Y2K report card (www.house.gov/reform/gmit) and articles written by Y2K experts Peter de Jaeger (www.year2000.com), Tony Keyes (www.y2kinvestor.com), and Michael Hyatt (www.michaelhyatt.com). Also, consider including *Newsweek*'s cover story on Y2K (June 2, 1997) and, of course, a copy of this book.

Show the benefits of preparedness. Do not just focus on Y2K during your first conversation. It is wise to briefly touch on natural disasters that have affected your community over the years and what could happen in the future. If your spouse is reluctant to talk about Y2K, he or she will be much more willing to talk about storms, floods, and fires. It is a good idea if you assemble a stack of newspaper stories on crises that have happened in your state—it validates your concern and stirs your spouse's memory of past disasters.

Don't be upset (or surprised) if your spouse decides to dwell on natural disasters. That is to be expected. He or she is dealing with a *known* threat, something that he or she is familiar with and, quite likely, has personally endured. By contrast, Y2K is a global technological threat—one that no one has ever experienced.

If your spouse is reluctant to even discuss natural disaster planning, then you need to be more firm. Sometimes, saying something like, "But doesn't it make sense to be prepared for these things? I mean, don't we owe it to ourselves and our children to be proactive? I don't want to see any of us get hurt," makes a big difference.

That is called *guilt*. It usually works like a charm when all other methods fail.

Don't expect anything . . . initially. How your spouse reacts to your concern about Y2K will depend on several factors, including: 1) his or her knowledge of the year 2000 crisis; 2) his or her prior encounters with natural disasters; 3) whether you live in a city or rural environment; and 4) what resources, financial and otherwise, you have available to you.

Not surprisingly, individuals who are more knowledgeable about Y2K are less resistant to making preparations for it. Likewise, people who have weathered severe weather before— tornadoes, hurricanes, wildfires, earthquakes—are willing to take action. (Your spouse may actually surprise you. He or she may have the same concerns as you do but was afraid to raise the topic.)

Compromise on what you will and will not discuss. This is an often overlooked aspect of crisis communications. You must realize that not everyone is comfortable talking about disasters. For some people there are certain topics that are considered to be off limits, such as death, starvation, or the use of weapons for self-defense.

Thus, you need to ask your spouse (and, eventually, your children) what limitations he or she would like to establish as far as conversation topics are concerned. Once the limits are known, honor them.

I know of one family, for instance, that has successfully established its Y2K boundaries. The wife asked her husband to share information with her in small chunks. She felt she could handle only one issue at a time. If she tried to deal with multiple issues and tasks simultaneously, it would overwhelm and possibly panic her. It was also agreed that neither parent would discuss apocalyptic scenarios in front of their children. And neither would they talk about the possibility of having to put down their pets if they became injured or if they were starving to death.

Don't argue. There are two issues that couples tend to disagree over: first, how severe the millennium bug will be and, second, how much preparation should be taken. Please keep in mind that yelling never accomplishes anything. In fact, it only makes matters worse. When discussing Y2K preparedness, express your thoughts and concerns, and then shut up. Let your spouse mull your words over. If a disagreement arises, try to calmly negotiate your way through it. You are not at war with your family. You are simply trying to make sure you have all the things you need for your family's safety, protection, and comfort. Arguing only distracts everyone involved from the real issue at hand: preparing for a possible emergency.

TIP 6 *Build a survival library.*

Pretend for a moment that you have gone for a hike in the woods and that you are lost. Worse, it is pouring rain—

SPIKE DATES FOR 1999

The millennium bug is not just a January 1, 2000, problem. There are a number of other dates that could cause trouble. Many of them occur in 1999, the transition year for Y2K. Here are just a few problems that were reported after computers rolled over from 1998 to 1999:

- On New Year's Eve, Lynn Electric (Bluefield, WV)—a remanufacturer of generators and motors—was unable to close its annual payroll records and open a 1999 file on its Act Plus accounting software. All the computer documents reverted to 1944, a date sometimes used by software programmers as the start date for operating system clocks.
- On January 4, 1999—the first business day of the year—a brand-new computer-driven security system refused to open the locked doors of Sterling and Sterling Insurance (Long Island, NY) for about half the company's employees.
- PCS Health Systems, Inc. (Scottsdale, AZ), which manages drug benefits for 3.7 million federal employees and retirees, accidentally disqualified many of them from buying prescriptions on New Year's Eve. When midnight struck, a computer began denying drug authorizations. Over the next 20 hours, 96,531 members at some 47,000 pharmacies nationwide were turned down before the problem was finally fixed.
- Environmental Systems Products in Bohemia, NY, which supplies auto emission-testing equipment, was shocked to learn that its equipment could not produce a 00 windshield sticker for drivers whose cars had passed inspection. (The 00 represents the expiration date for the year 2000.) Instead, the equipment printed out stickers marked 91. Many inspection stations simply put them on car windows without looking at them. As a result, police began ticketing the apparently out-of-date cars. It took the company nearly two weeks to correct the problem.
- As mentioned earlier in this book, 11 states were temporarily unable to generate unemployment payment checks on January 4, 1999. Some states had to write the checks by hand.
- In late January, Prodigy Communications Corp. announced that it was shutting down its Prodigy Classic on-line service.

They cited Y2K problems as being the cause, but declined to go into details. The closure affects more than 208,000 Prodigy Classic subscribers.

And here is a list of "spike dates" to keep an eye out for:

January 1, 1999—Rollover date that could affect computers that maintain forward-looking documents a full year in advance, such as unemployment benefits and insurance policies.

April 1, 1999—Start of New York's fiscal year (FY) 2000. It is also the start of the Canadian and Japanese fiscal year.

April 6, 1999—The beginning of England's FY 2000.

April 9, 1999—The 99th day of the 99th year (Julian calendar), which is represented as 9999 in some computer programs. Historically, 9999 was used by programmers as a "shut-off" or "stop" command.

July 1, 1999—The beginning of FY 2000 in 46 states.

August 21, 1999—The global positioning satellite (GPS) system time rolls over. Unless repaired, many GPS receivers will claim that it is January 6, 1980, on August 22; January 7, 1980, on August 23; etc.

September 1, 1999—Start of Texas's FY 2000.

September 9, 1999—The date is a minefield of 9s.

September 9, 1999—The 99th day in the Gregorian calendar (i.e., 9999).

October 1999—Three-month financial projections incorporate the year 2000.

October 1, 1999—The start of the U.S. government's FY 2000, as well as Michigan's and Alabama's.

January 1, 2000—First day of the century (01/01/00). The date rollover will halt, confuse, or disrupt many systems and devices.

January 3, 2000—First business day of the century.

January 10, 2000—First day requiring a seven-digit field.

February 29, 2000—Some systems will not recognize leap year.

October 10, 2000—First day requiring an eight-digit field, the maximum length.

December 31, 2000—Some systems using Julian calendar dates may not recognize the 366th day of the leap year.

February 29, 2004—Another leap year.

you are soaking wet and becoming hypothermic. Fortunately for you, though, you find a book of matches in your hip pack. The bad news is that there are only three matches left and two of them are wet.

Now for the big question: Do you know how to build a fire with just one match? Are you sure? Are you willing to bet your life on it?

Knowledge is power, and knowledge can keep you alive. That is why I encourage you—if you have not already done so—to establish an in-house library of books and documents that you can refer to in an emergency situation. Important topics and subtopics that you should consider having in your bookcase include:

animal husbandry
engine repair
food
    canning and drying
    cookbooks
    edible wild plants
    food preparation
    food safety
    woodstove cooking
gardening
health and medicine
    alternative/natural medicine
    child health
    first aid
    dental care
    sanitation and hygiene
    vitamin supplementation
home
    carpentry
    electrical
    home repair
    plumbing
sewing

    survival
        communications
        compass navigation
        hunting and trapping
        map reading
        plant identification
        weaponscraft
        wilderness survival skills
    water
        purification
        sources
    weather

A good used bookstore can provide you with a plethora of inexpensive books to fill these categories. To get a head start on your search, refer to Appendix 3 for a few recommended titles. Make certain that your library includes user's manuals and repair guides for any appliances and survival equipment you may own, such as propane heaters, gas stoves, generators, and lanterns. You may also want to include how-to brochures

---

CHECK IT OUT . . . YOURSELF

Y2K poll
   www.jsonline.com/bym/tech/0126survey.asp

Dealing with a nonbelieving spouse
   www.MrsWomen.com
   www.y2kwomen.com

Survival how-to document library
   forums.cosmoaccess.net/forum/survival/prep/survival.htm

Disaster handbook
   www.foodsafety.org/dbhome.htm

Global outlooks
   www.globalmf.org
   www.worldbank.org/y2k
   www.global2k.com

from various organizations and state/federal agencies, such as the American Red Cross, Department of Agriculture, FEMA, and the Centers for Disease Control and Prevention.

And last, if you have children, by all means add school books and recreational titles to the library. There is absolutely no reason why education has to stop just because of the millennium bug.

TIP   *7*   ***Assess what resources you have, and what you need.***

Turn the page . . .

Remember:
Hope for the best, prepare for the worst!
Prudence, <u>not</u> panic!

Getting Started

ASSESS WHAT YOU HAVE AND WHAT YOU NEED

> The year 2000 problem is real;
> its consequences are serious;
> and the deadline remains unstoppable.
> —Congressman Stephen Horn (R-CA)
> February 22, 1999

> Our safety is not in blindness,
> but in facing our dangers.
> —Schiller, *The Sublime*

TIP 8 *Take an inventory*.

Why take an inventory? The answer is quite simple: you need to know what you already have so you can figure out what you need to buy or acquire for an emergency. You don't want to duplicate what you already have; to do so would be a waste of money. As you list the inventory, you will be surprised by what you own—items hidden away in drawers, closets, and cabinets that you have forgotten about.

So how do you create the inventory?

Step 1: Assault every room in your house or apartment, one room at a time, and explore every nook and cranny (including closets, boxes, and storage containers). Write down on paper what items, and how much of each item, are found.

If you do this correctly, it will take you about thirty minutes to do a single room. (Faster if your spouse and children help.) Bathrooms, kitchens, basements, crawl spaces, sheds, garages, barns, and attics take much longer—upward of one to two hours depending on their size and how much stuff you crammed away in them.

Be patient with this effort. Spread it out over a few days if you have to, but don't give up. You really do need to know what belongings you have. It will help you figure out what you are lacking and what you need to buy (and, more important, in what priority). It will also give you a clear idea of what items you have that, if necessary, you could sell to raise money or barter away for a much-needed item.

Step 2: Take your multiple lists when you are finished and sit down at a table. Now, compile all the information under common subcategories such as clothing, shoes, canned food, tools, cooking utensils, camping gear, and gardening items. This will give you an overall idea of what your family owns.

When you are done with this task, take these numerous subcategories and place them in file folders marked:

Water
Food/Basic Supplies
Sanitation, Health, and Medicine
Power, Heat, Lighting, Communications, and
    Transportation
Personal Safety
Financial and Legal

Why should you bother to do this? Because each of these major topics is a chapter in this book! Hence, you will be able to take your file folders quickly and (easily) compare them with the recommended lists found in each of these chapters. This will give you a good idea of what items you have plenty of and what items you are lacking or short on.

Step 3: Review each file folder, highlighting the items that you deem to be critical. By critical, I mean your health or safety would be at risk if the item was not available. For instance, a first-aid kit (found in the Sanitation, Health, and Medicine file) is a critical item. Without it, you could bleed to death from a severe cut before an ambulance arrives Likewise, a fire extinguisher (found in the Personal Safety file) is also be a critical item. Without it, your house could burn down if there is a grease fire in the kitchen.

By contrast, clocks are generally not critical items. (An

exception would be if a clock is used to alert someone to take time-sensitive medications.) Similarly, houseplants are not critical items, and neither are paintings, tables, and chairs. You could survive without them if you had to.

List every item you have marked as being critical on a separate piece of paper.

Step 4: Look at your Critical Items list. Recall from Chapter 1 that there are four major crises the millennium bug could cause: power outages, distribution problems, financial meltdown, and war. Of these, the loss of power has the most immediate and severe effect on your family. Within hours, especially if it is in the middle of winter, you will be freezing cold unless you take precautions.

If any critical item is electrical in nature, place a big red *E* next to it on the list. It signifies that you *must* find an alternative for it. For example, if your heating furnace operates on electricity, then you have to find another way to generate heat (e.g., woodstove, propane/kerosene heater, fireplace insert) or to stay warm (e.g., goose-down clothing, chemical heating pads).

Go back through the critical list again, this time placing a green $ next to anything that could be adversely affected by the lack of money (i.e., financial meltdown). Food and fuel will assuredly be two of the items you will mark. If you have no money, you can't buy either of these. Thus, you could starve or freeze to death if the economy doesn't straighten out quickly. You need to consider stockpiling these at-risk items.

Go through the list one last time, placing a blue ✈ next to any item that will be affected if there is a national distribution crisis. (The ✈ represents a plane, which is part of the transportation system.) This is easy to figure out if you just ask yourself, "What could I run out of?" Top candidates include food, heating fuel (e.g., oil, propane), and emergency energy sources (e.g., batteries).

Now, what about war, the last of the possible Y2K crises? Why didn't I have you go through the list placing little ✳ bomb blasts next to items that would be affected by war? Well, because you have already labeled those items. Anything marked with a $ or ✈ is a war item.

Step 5: Physical household items aside, you also need to assess your finances and investments. For instance, how much loose money do you have in the house? How much do you have in your bank accounts? IRAs? Other retirement accounts? Savings accounts? Investments? If any of these can be withdrawn—even if there is a penalty—mark it down on paper. These are your emergency reserves.

What valuables do you own (e.g., jewelry, collectibles, art, coins)? These could be sold or traded for desperately needed items. Hence, they need to be protected.

How much do you owe in credit card debt? Mortgage? Home equity loans? Student loans? Car payments? Other installment payments? These are your liabilities. You will be expected to pay these even if there is a national crisis. If you don't, you could stand to lose your home. You could also be forced into bankruptcy, which jeopardizes all your other belongings.

Step 6: Assess your skills and abilities. Do you have special skills that you could make a living on or barter with if things in the world get really bad? For example, do you have any training or hands-on experience as a carpenter, upholsterer, plumber, electrician, mechanic, photographer, seamstress, gardener, doctor, and so on? If so, it could come in handy some day.

If you don't have any skills, then now at least you know it and can take steps to learn a trade that will benefit your family.

Step 7: The only thing remaining to do is for you to take a walk around your house or apartment again. This time note where all the utilities (e.g., water, sewage, electric) enter the structure and where the emergency shut-off valves are located. This is very important.

For example, suppose you live in a house out in the countryside where your sewage is pumped uphill to an underground septic tank. If the power goes out, the sewage is going to follow gravity's pull and flow right back into your house!

Unless you shut the flow valve, you are going to have a huge mess on your hands.

Likewise, if the power goes out and the oil pipes in your basement freeze and crack, you are going to have oil all over the place. Then, when the power finally kicks back on, turning on your furnace, you could have an explosion or flash fire. Again, knowing where the shut-off valve is located can prevent a disaster like this from happening.

TIP 9 *Make a preparedness plan*.

Pat yourself on the back! You now have a better understanding of your personal assets and liabilities than the majority of people in America do. You have taken the first major step to being prepared for a disaster, whether it is caused by severe weather or Y2K. Now it is time to create a realistic and practical plan that will enable you to be "disaster ready."

First, you must establish a direction and some goals for yourself and your family:

1. What are you striving to achieve with your preparedness efforts? In other words, do you want to be completely or partly self-sufficient? Define self-sufficient so that everyone in the family is crystal clear as to what you are all working toward.
2. How much food, fuel, water, clothing, and so forth will you stockpile? A three-day supply? A week? A month? Three months? Half a year? A full year? More?
3. How much money will you set aside as an emergency cash reserve? And, more important, how will you accumulate this amount? Will you set aside $50 out of every paycheck, for instance? Will you simply designate an existing bank account as being the emergency fund? Or will you sell personal belongings to raise the money?
4. How much time are you giving yourself to stockpile

needed goods and money? When do you want to be completely done with your preparedness efforts?

5. What strategy will you use to acquire needed goods? For instance, when food shopping, are you going to buy duplicates of everything? Or are you going to wait until the needed items are on sale and then buy in large quantities? Will you rely on local stores for your emergency supplies, or will you use wholesalers or mail-order companies?

6. What essential training do you and your family members need to receive (e.g., first aid, sewing, wilderness survival, fire fighting, gardening, animal husbandry)? When must it be completed by? (Note: FEMA has free courses on disaster preparedness. Go to www.fema.gov/emi/ishome. htm or call your nearest FEMA office, which will be listed in the telephone directory under Government, United States.)

Once you and your family have discussed these questions, you can continue with the plan. In the second portion, outline how you will deal with the following issues. Consider this to be a brainstorming session. Gather the family in the living room and then toss out one of these subjects for their consideration. The questions posed here are not inclusive—they are simply provided to jump-start your creativity and to get your mind in gear.

Heat—How will you stay warm if the electricity goes out? What other forms of heating are available to you? Should you winterize your home or apartment? If so, what needs to be done (e.g., pipe insulation, window blankets)?

Safety—How will you prevent fires from happening? What will you use to put out a fire? Should you get battery-operated smoke detectors? Are there any carbon monoxide dangers in your home? How secure is the house from intruders? What security measures can you add (e.g., dead bolt, battery-powered lighting)? Should you have firearms in the house for hunting or personal protection? Are there other forms of self-defense that should be considered instead of firearms?

Power—What alternatives are available to you to generate electricity (e.g., solar power, fuel cells, generator, battery, wind/water power)? If you opt for a generator, how much fuel will you need to stockpile and do you have adequate safe storage for it? How will you get the power to specific appliances in your home?

Cooking—What will you use to cook your food (e.g., propane stove)? How many burners will you need? How much fuel will you need to cook two to three meals a day? Do you have adequate and safe storage for it?

Communications—If an emergency arises, how will you call for help? Whom will you call for help? Do you want a radio available to monitor conditions? If so, how will it be powered?

Sanitation—How will you launder your dirty clothes and clean your dishes? What will you use for a toilet? How will you dispose of the waste and where? How will you combat insect and rodent infestations? How will you take a shower, and how often?

Clothing—What clothing do you need to stay warm in the winter and comfortable in the summer? What footwear will need replacing in the near future as a result of wear and tear or growth? How will you repair worn or torn clothing?

Food—How much food will you stockpile? Where will you store it? How will you prevent food from spoiling? How many calories per day will you restrict your dietary intake to?

Water—How much water will you stockpile? Where will you store it, and in what kind of containers? What methods will you use to purify the water? What sources of water are near your home?

Financial—What types of financial and legal records should you keep in a file (e.g., bank statements, mutual fund updates, tax returns, credit report)? How much cash will you keep in the home for emergencies, and where will you safely store it? If you lose your job, how will you earn a living? If banks begin limiting withdrawal amounts, how will you address it?

Light—What alternate forms of lighting will you use (e.g., candles, propane/kerosene lanterns, flashlights, chemical glow sticks)? Under what conditions will you allow them to be used?

Transportation—If the distribution system crashes and the country's gas and oil supplies dwindle, how will you get around? Will you walk, use bicycles, or resort to horse and buggy?

Medical—What prescriptions and vitamin supplements will you stockpile and how will you keep them safely stored? What medical records are you going to get copies of and where will you keep them filed? What immunizations will you get? Will you get training in emergency medicine?

Pets—What items will you stockpile for your pets (e.g., food, vitamins, prescriptions)? How much water will you store for their daily needs? Where will you store all of this? How will you keep your pets warm? What will you do with their waste?

Parents—If a parent lives with you, what are his/her special needs? Are there disabilities or medical conditions that you need to be aware of and prepared for? What are his/her expectations of you and the family during a crisis?

Children—If you have young children in the home, what are their special needs? How will you keep them entertained? If school closes, will you teach them yourself or hire a tutor?

TIP ⏻10 *Establish priorities.*

How you actually prepare for a disaster depends on several things, including your level of anxiety and what fears you have, how much money and free time you have, the number of people you have to make preparations for, where you live, what resources are readily available to you, how skilled you are as a handyman, and what dire Y2K consequences you are anticipating.

When you review your preparedness plan, you may feel overwhelmed. There appear to be so many things that need to be done, and indeed there are. So where do you begin?

Base your decision on your current home inventory. For

instance, since the millennium bug will arrive in the middle of winter, staying warm will be a priority for you. (This is especially true if you live in northern climes.) But if you already have a woodstove or a propane heater, you don't have to worry about purchasing one. Yours will work just fine if the power goes out. Thus, another survival topic will become a higher priority for you, such as making sure that you have an adequate fuel supply so the stove or heater can keep going.

Your highest priority should be to address the items found on your Critical Items list. Focus first on items that have all three symbols (E, $, and ✈) next to them. This is because they will be influenced by any and all of the four millennium bug crises that were mentioned in Chapter 1.

Your next priority should be those items marked with an *E*. Power blackouts occur quite often, even in the absence of the millennium bug.

And last, address those critical items marked by $, followed by those marked with a ✈. When you are done with the items on the Critical Items list, you can move on to less essential actions, knowing that you are now ready to meet any crisis head-on.

TIP 11 *Figure out your buying strategy*.

Establishing a well-equipped, in-home emergency stockpile is not an inexpensive proposition. It takes money (or strong bartering skills) to create and maintain it. That is why you and your spouse must seriously discuss how you will buy your supplies. There are several ways to do this:

1. Keep an eye out for store sales. When you see that an item on your "buy" list is on sale, purchase it in quantity.
2. When doing your normal, weekly food shopping, buy duplicates of nonperishable foods for your emergency stockpile.
3. Buy in bulk. There are a number of stores (e.g., Sam's

Club, Cosco) that specialize in bulk item sales. You generally get more for the money than if you bought the items at a local retail store.

4. Shop for durable goods you need (e.g., woodstove, generator, storage containers) at auctions, pawnshops, yard sales, flea markets, street sales, and consignment shops. Newspaper ads are another source of inexpensive items. You can also check out Internet auction sites. One of the largest and best known is eBay (www.ebay.com), which typically lists 900,000 + items for sale at any given time.

How do you get the money to buy items? Well, there are a couple of ways. First, you can set aside $50 to $100 from each paycheck and use that. Second, you can dip into your savings accounts. Third, you can clean out your closets, basement, and garage and have a huge yard sale. Fourth, you can pawn your valuables. Fifth, you can cash in your savings bonds or other investment vehicles. And sixth, you can sell your skills (e.g., yard work, upholstery, photography, engine repair) to people who need them.

Regardless of how you raise your money, do not take a cash advance on your credit card or get a bank loan to finance your emergency provisions. Why? For a few reasons. One is that credit-card cash advances generally have higher interest rates than your normal card. Why should you pay more?

Another reason is that if, for instance, you lose your job as a result of a Y2K problem, you may find it impossible to pay your monthly bills. Defaulting on your credit card debt or bank loan will not only ruin your credit, but it can result in bankruptcy and the loss of your home and personal belongings.

TIP ▶ 12 *Figure out where you are going to store provisions.*

Before you run out and start buying emergency provisions, figure out where you are going to store all of it first.

Food, water, and fuel take up a tremendous amount of space, especially if you intend to have a month's worth of provisions on hand, or more!

To illustrate this, if you bought a one-year food supply for one person from a mail-order company, your UPS driver would deliver 30 cartons containing 182 No. 10–sized cans. The boxes would weigh some 600 pounds and occupy 42 cubic feet. That is for just *one person*! Multiply that figure by the number of people in your home and you'll quickly understand why adequate storage can be a significant problem.

Also, note that this example does *not* include water, fuels, or basic survival supplies! They take up additional space.

So you must determine where you are going to store your emergency reserves. In the northern region of the United States, most houses have a full basement. It makes for an ideal storage space, especially if it is not too damp. Why? A basement is generally cool and dark. These conditions actually extend the life of canned food items and packaged dry provisions.

Unfortunately, if you live in the deep South, your home is probably built on a cement slab. If luck is smiling on you at all, though, you may have a crawl space available to you. If so, use it.

Attics and sheds are much too hot for food storage. In fact, they shorten the life of canned goods. They are also too hot for fuel storage. Propane tanks, for instance, only have a 20 percent expansion allowance. If you store these tanks in a hot shed, they'll blow. For this reason, your best bet for storage may be a drafty barn or a large shed built under some shade trees.

If you live in cave country, you may want to give some consideration to storing items in a nearby cave. Like a basement, it is dark and cool. Just be extremely careful of snakes, rabid bats, wild animals occupying the cave, and, of course, falling rocks.

For those of you who live in an apartment, space is usually at a premium. Therefore you may not be able to store as many supplies as you want. Consider storing your provisions in closets, under a stairwell, in the coat closet, under beds and couches, et cetera.

If you have a good friend who lives in a nearby house, ask if you can store the bulk of your supplies there. In return, you can share some of your reserves with him or her when a disaster strikes. Another idea is to rent space at a storage facility and park your supplies there. (For food storage, make sure the shed is climate controlled.) If you take this route: 1) do not store fuels or explosives; 2) buy and use a good padlock; and 3) pack your belongings in unmarked boxes so that curious bystanders do not know you are stocking emergency supplies.

Space limitations aside, apartment renters may also be hindered by weight considerations. This is especially true if your apartment is located in a very old house or building. From a structural standpoint, it may not be able to withstand the additional 1,200 pounds that you plunk down. So beware.

TIP 13 *Talk with your children and include them in the preparations.*

At some point you need to bring your children, if you have any, into the discussion on emergency preparedness. I feel that the best time to do this is after you and your spouse have reached a mutual agreement about Y2K—how bad it will be, and what course of action you are going to take to minimize its impact. By waiting until then, you will present a united front to the children. If you both are in agreement, it will only serve to reassure the rest of the household.

What do you tell them? It depends on their age. For young children, tell them you are going to take precautions against bad storms, like what they see on television. "By doing this," you say, "we can make sure that we'll all be safe."

For older children, who generally understand computer technology, be open and honest with them: "We are worried that the year 2000 computer glitch might knock out the power. So we're going to take some precautions, just in case. Even if

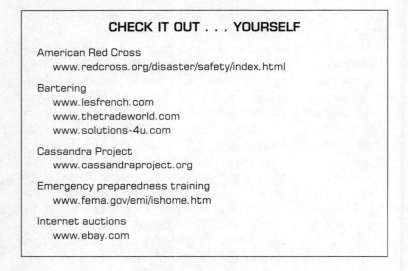

CHECK IT OUT . . . YOURSELF

American Red Cross
    www.redcross.org/disaster/safety/index.html

Bartering
    www.lesfrench.com
    www.thetradeworld.com
    www.solutions-4u.com

Cassandra Project
    www.cassandraproject.org

Emergency preparedness training
    www.fema.gov/emi/ishome.htm

Internet auctions
    www.ebay.com

nothing happens, we will still be ready for _____ [list a natural disaster that strikes your area of the country]."

In either instance, it is a good idea to ask your children what they think about taking precautions. Doing so helps them process the information. It also shows that you value their opinion, that they are not going to be ignored.

TIP 14 *Divvy up the responsibilities.*

Emergency preparedness not only goes much faster with more people involved but it has the added benefit that many different brains are making suggestions that one person would have overlooked or never thought of. So, when you begin making preparations, it is a wise idea to spread the responsibilities among your family members.

When doing this, try to match a person's natural interest with the task at hand. For example, if your 17-year-old daughter has a strong interest in backpacking, then ask her to compile a list of suggested camping items you should purchase. If your 11-year-old son loves to read, ask him to oversee the in-house survival library. If your spouse is concerned about heating issues, ask him or her to investigate what alternatives there are to keep the family warm if a power outage occurs.

TIP 15 *Have a brief, weekly meeting.*

It makes sense to get together. You need to know what has been accomplished in the past seven days and what your family needs to focus on for the upcoming week. The meeting also permits everyone to brainstorm, share ideas, and critique existing efforts.

By all means, try to keep these meetings short—an hour or less. No one enjoys a looooooong meeting where legs, rear ends, and brains go numb. If you have children involved in the discussions, their interest will vanish at around 30 minutes. So if you anticipate a long meeting, let them know up front and have them give their progress report first, if they have one to present.

Water

We must recognize that this problem is coming and that it must
be dealt with coldly, intelligently and efficiently. Don't panic, but
don't spend a lot of time sleeping, either.
—Senator Bob Bennett (R-UT)

According to a U.S. Senate report released at the end of February 1999, only half of America's electric utilities had repaired their Y2K systems. The report concluded that local and regional blackouts are likely. ("Of greatest concern are about 1,000 small, rural utilities.")

As you know, when you lose electricity, you lose your water, even if you live out in the country and have a well. That's because it requires a pump to draw the water up from the underground reservoir. If you are fortunate to have a shallow well—say only 20 feet deep or so—you can rely on muscles, sweat, and a hand pump to get to your water supply. But for the rest of us, we are going to have to find alternate water reserves to get by on.

Thus, your *first goal* is to establish an adequate supply of water. Why water and not food? Because without water, you can die within a week . . . regardless of how much food you stockpile or what fancy survival equipment you have stashed away.

As soon as you are cut off from a supply of fresh water, you begin to dehydrate. How fast you lose water depends on a number of factors: how much water your body already contains, the ambient temperature, altitude, the clothing you wear, your level of physical exertion, how nervous you are, whether or not you are in direct sunlight, et cetera. When you lose 1 or 2 percent of your body weight to dehydration, you feel thirsty. By the time you lose 5 percent, however, you have a headache and feel weak and nauseous. You will also have lost your appetite. At 10 percent, you have slurred speech, breathing problems, and you won't be able to walk. You will feel a tingling sensation in your limbs. And finally, at 12 to 15 percent, you collapse and die.

So for your body and vital organs to function properly, you must replace water that you lose. This is why your first priority in preparing for Y2K is to establish an adequate and safe reserve of water. Fortunately, water is the cheapest emergency item to acquire—it is often just a twist of the faucet away!—and the easiest to store. However, realize that water also weighs more—eight pounds per gallon—and it takes up more space. So plan appropriately.

TIP 16 *Have an adequate stockpile of water.*

The average person drinks about half a gallon of water every day—more if he or she is very active and if the weather is warm. At the very minimum, you should figure on stockpiling one gallon of water per person per day. Two gallons is a much better figure, though. Having the extra water available for each person allows for unexpected strenuous activities as well as for brushing teeth, hand washing, and other sanitary activities.

Two gallons may not sound like a lot to you, and you are quite right, it isn't. On any given day, most of us swim and guzzle our way through an amazing 150 gallons of water as we go through our normal routines—showers, toilet flushings, cooking, dish washing, and laundry. So to suddenly reduce this water use by 148 gallons is indeed a shocking act.

But remember, we are talking about surviving a disaster. In this environment, you will be as happy as a pig in mud that you even have any water to use and drink. Used judiciously, two gallons of water a day will go quite far.

Exactly how much water should you stockpile? Well, first you need to figure out how many gallons you need for a single day. Use this equation:

Number of family members _____ x 2 gallons per person = _____

Now, multiply that number by 14 days. The total is how much drinking water you need for a two-week period—the amount I recommend. (Note: A 30-day supply is recommended for those who have adequate storage space.) For a family of four, this equates to 112 gallons of water. For a family of five, it's 140 gallons.

When determining your water needs, don't forget your pets! They need clean drinking water, too.

HOW DEHYDRATED ARE YOU?

The most common symptoms of dehydration are: low urine output, dark-colored urine that has a strong odor, fatigue, sunken eyes, and loss of skin elasticity. If you are thirsty, you are already 2 percent dehydrated.

You can estimate how much fluid a person has lost by using his pulse and breathing rates as a guide. The higher the rates, the greater the fluid loss:

¾ Quart Loss
    Pulse: 100 beats or less per minute
    Breathing rate: 12–20 per minute

¾ to 1½ Quarts Loss
    Pulse: 100–120 beats per minute
    Breathing rate: 20–30 per minute

1½ to 2 Quarts Loss
    Pulse: 120–140 beats per minute
    Breathing Rate: 30–40 per minute

Source: U.S. Army

Should you store more water than for a 14-day supply? Well, certainly, if you feel compelled to do so and, more important, if you have the space for it. Since water cannot be compressed, it takes up a lot of space. For example, if you use five-gallon containers for storage, a family of five will have 28 jugs to contend with. That's for a two-week supply. Increase it to a three-month reserve, and you will be dealing with 168 containers—the total weight of which would be 6,720 pounds!

To get off to a quick start on your water stockpile, visit your local grocery store and purchase some bottled water. Most generic store brands cost $.50 per gallon. You can pick up six gallons per family member to give you a three-day supply. It will only cost $3 per person . . . or $1 a day. This will give you peace of mind until you are able to begin stockpiling your main water reserve.

TIP 17 *Store water from the source you are currently drinking.*

This approach makes sense if for only one reason: you and your family are accustomed to the water's taste. If you were to get your water from another source—say, for instance, a bottled-water manufacturer—you may not like the way it tastes when you finally open up the barrels in an emergency. Guess what? You won't drink as much of it, even though you know you should. That means you may eventually become dehydrated.

TIP 18 *Store your water in clean plastic containers with tight-fitting lids.*

There are a number of containers on today's market that you can put water in, including 5-gallon jugs, 7-gallon stackable containers, 30-gallon tanks, and 55-gallon drums. In selecting the container size, keep in mind that when full of water, it will be heavy. For instance, a 5-gallon container will weigh 40 pounds; a 30-gallon tank, 240 pounds. If you have to move the containers around by yourself or if you think you may have to evacuate the area for some reason, then buy and use the smaller containers. Your arms and back will thank you for it.

Any water container that you do end up using should have an airtight lid so that bacteria and other contaminants cannot get inside and spoil the water. (Make sure you add bleach to the water for long-term storage. The bleach will kill any organisms in the water, making it safe to drink.)

If you purchase large water barrels—15 gallons in size and larger—buy a self-priming siphon pump to draw the water out. A plastic universal pump typically sells for $15 to $20. A bung wrench ($10) is another item you should consider purchasing: it quickly removes caps from these barrels without busting your knuckles in the process.

Have a variety of different size water containers on hand. For your primary water stockpile, you may want to go with 15-, 30-, or 55-gallon drums but, for ease of use and portability, buy several 5- or 7-gallon containers. These smaller containers often have built-in, molded carrying handles and spigots. Several are also designed so that they are stackable—a blessing if you don't have a lot of storage space.

Here are some other valuable guidelines for you to keep in mind:

- Don't use plastic containers that once held foodstuffs (i.e., the thin plastic containers that are so often used to store mustard, ketchup, pickles, and milk). The plastic in these containers often retains the taste and smell of its previous contents, which may contaminate any water you store in it. Also, these containers may burst apart if you drop them. If, however, you want to use these containers to store water for *nondrinking* purposes (e.g., washing), then by all means go ahead.
- Purify all your drinking water with bleach before storing it, especially if the water has come from an untreated source (e.g., lake, river).

- Don't use metal containers: They can impart an unpleasant taste to the water. Also, if the container is not coated inside with a special enamel or plastic, the water will rust the can.
- Store the water in a cool, dark place: it helps prevent bacteria from growing in the water. A basement or crawl space is perfect for storage.
- Store the water containers away from paint and petroleum-based products. Plastic containers like nalgene are porous, allowing strong odors to pass through and contaminate the water.
- Thoroughly sterilize empty water containers before filling them back up. This prevents illness and slime buildup.
- Label your containers. Place a two-by-three-inch label or a strip of masking tape on every container. On it, record the date the container was filled, where you got the water from, and what purification method was used to treat the water. This information will later help you identify which containers need to be used first. And, if you should become ill, it will help health authorities determine the possible source (e.g., lake, river, well) of the bacteria or parasite that caused your ailment.
- Some people complain that stored water tastes flat. You can overcome this by mixing the water with Kool-Aid or instant ice-tea mix. (Note: This is done *after* the water is poured out of the container.)

TIP 19 *Do not ration your water!*

It is common for people to ration their belongings in an emergency. That is because they don't know how long the crisis will last and they don't know if they have enough supplies on hand to see them through to the end.

Now, there are many things you can ration in an emergency (e.g., food, money), but water is not one of them. As mentioned earlier, your body needs water to maintain its vital functions. If you scrimp on the water, you are only hurting yourself. In fact, you could very well die from dehydration.

Thus, drink as much water as you can, when you can. Do not wait to drink until you feel thirsty. By then, you are already dehydrated. Instead, replace the water as you lose it. For the average person, this means drinking *at least* a gallon of water each day.

When disaster strikes and you open the first water container, immediately begin efforts to collect and purify water to refill the container once it is finally empty. This way, you will always have a two weeks' supply of water on hand.

If, for some reason, water becomes scarce, do the following: 1) Restrict your intake of food. Food requires water for digestion. 2) Conserve your fluids by reducing physical exertion. 3) Stay out of the heat and direct sunlight.

TIP 20 *Purify water before drinking it.*

You should *never* drink untreated water, no matter how crystal clear it may look to you. That is because bacteria and viruses that cause disease could very well be present. Some of the more common ailments that you can contract from drinking dirty water include: giardiasis, salmonellosis, cryptosporidiosis, typhoid, and cholera. There are also a host of waterborne worms, flukes, and leeches that could cause illness. And to make matters worse, many rivers, lakes, and ponds—from which you may one day get your water—are contaminated with animal feces.

So purify all water that will be used for drinking purposes. This includes water used to brush your teeth. Fortunately, there are a number of methods you can use to treat your water. This book examines three water-treatment methods: boiling, bleach disinfection, and iodine disinfection. There are other techniques, which are described in wilderness survival manuals, such as those printed by the U.S. military services. (Note: A fourth water-treatment method—ceramic water filtration—is discussed in Tip 21.)

When doing any of the following purification methods, it is a good idea to strain the water first through a cloth. Doing so removes a good portion of the sand, dirt, insect parts, twigs, and debris that might be in the water.

Boiling—This is the most universal and least technical method of taking care of dirty water. Place the water in a covered pot, bring it to a rolling boil, and then let it continue to boil for another 10 minutes. (Make sure the pot is covered or you will lose most of your water to evaporation!)

Some people complain that boiled water tastes flat. To improve the water's taste, aerate it: pour the water from one clean container to another several times before drinking it. Adding a small pinch of salt to each quart of boiled water also helps the taste if aeration alone does not.

Although boiling is easy to do, it does require a large amount of fuel. You may have to burn 5 to 10 minutes of propane just to bring the water to a boil, and add on another 10 minutes to purify the water. Using 15 to 20 minutes' worth of propane fuel may not sound like a lot, but if you purify water three times a day like this, day in and day out, it could put a serious dent in your fuel supply. You need to factor this in if you decide to use boiling as your primary water-treatment method.

Bleach Disinfection—This is a very simple method of killing any organisms in your water. You can use any household bleach containing **sodium hypochlorite** (5.25% solution), *as long as it does not have any soap additives or phosphates! Sodium hypochlorite must be the only active ingredient listed on the label!* Use an eyedropper or measuring spoon—the selection will depend on how much water you are disinfecting—to add the bleach to the water in the amount shown in Chart 4-1. Thoroughly mix the water and then allow it to stand for at least 30 minutes before drinking.

If you have done this process correctly, the water will have

CHART 4-1

BLEACH DISINFECTION

Water Amount	Water Condition	Amount of Bleach
1 Quart	Clear	2 drops
	Cloudy	4 drops
Half Gallon	Clear	4 drops
	Cloudy	8 drops
1 Gallon	Clear	8 drops
	Cloudy	16 drops
5 Gallons	Clear	½ teaspoon
	Cloudy	1 teaspoon

Source: FEMA

a distinct chlorine odor and taste, just like a swimming pool. If it does not, then add and mix in the same dose of the bleach to the water. Let it stand for another 20 minutes.

Iodine Disinfection—Although tincture of iodine (2 percent) can be used to purify water, you need to know that there are some drawbacks. First, pregnant or nursing women should *not* drink iodine-treated water and neither should people who have a thyroid problem. Second, iodine has a peculiar odor and taste, which many people find disagreeable. And last, iodine should only be used to purify *small* amounts of water—a gallon or less at a time.

Disinfecting water with iodine is similar to the process used for bleach. Add the iodine to the water in the quantities shown in Chart 4-2, mix thoroughly, and then let the solution stand for 30 minutes.

Purification Tablets—Many camping and outdoor retail stores sell water purification tablets (or liquids) to treat contaminated water. The majority of these products are either bleach or iodine based, with one or two tablets typically being used to purify a quart of water. Always follow the instructions on the package, and be aware that some of these products have

CHART 4-2

IODINE DISINFECTION

Water Amount	Water Condition	Amount of 2% Iodine
1 Quart	Clear	3 drops
	Cloudy	6 drops
Half Gallon	Clear	6 drops
	Cloudy	12 drops
1 Gallon	Clear	12 drops
	Cloudy	24 drops

Source: FEMA

an expiration date. Product examples include Polar Pure, Potable Aqua, and Micropur.

TIP 21 *Buy a water filtration system.*

At some point you may find it necessary to get water from a murky pond, roadside ditch, street puddle, sewage pipe, toilet bowl, etc. Who knows where that water has been and what might be lurking in it? (Actually I know, but we won't go there.) But, as you know, desperate times require desperate measures, so you won't turn your nose away from life-preserving water—no matter how it churns your stomach.

The big question is this: How do you treat it?

Well, first you have to get rid of all the filth in it. That's where a water filtration system comes in handy. There are several brands on today's market that you can select from—Pur, Katadyn, and MSR to name a few. For the most part, they all rely on ceramic cartridges with microscopic pores to filter out the bad stuff and allow the water to pass through. How fast this process works depends on the number of filters used and the intake pore size.

The Pur Scout ($90), for instance, measures 9 inches long

and 2.25 inches wide and weighs 12 ounces. It can treat up to 100 gallons of water at a pint per minute before the filter must be replaced. The intake pore size is 150 microns, which means you still have to boil or chemically treat the water since some forms of bacteria can still pass through.

By comparison, the Katadyn Pocket Filter ($250)—which is of similar dimensions as the Scout—can filter up to 13,000 gallons of water at a rate of one quart per minute before the filter must be replaced. Its filter pore size is a mere 0.2 microns, which effectively screens out all bacteria. You can drink the filtered water without further treatment! (For this reason, the Katadyn is the only purifier approved by the International Red Cross for fieldwork.)

If you don't have the financial means to purchase a filtration system like these, you can make your own. Take an old clean pair of pants and tie off one of the legs at the cuff. Partially fill that pant leg with sand, crushed rock, and charcoal/fireplace ashes to just below the knee. Suspend the pants from a low-hanging tree branch and place a clean bucket underneath. When you have dirty water that needs filtering, simply pour the water into the pant leg. The water will slowly filter through the ash/sand/rock layers and drip into the bucket.

Of course, all this does is make the water clear and a bit more palatable. *You still have to purify it by boiling or chemical disinfection.*

TIP 22 *Locate emergency sources of water.*

You never know what will happen. That is why you must identify alternate sources of water you can use in an emergency. This is particularly important for city residents since there are fewer natural water sources available to them than to people who live in rural America.

Here is a list of potential emergency water sources. It is far

---

CHECK IT OUT . . . YOURSELF

American Red Cross
   www.redcross.org/disaster/safety/index.html

American Water Works Association
   www.awwa.org/y2ksrvey.htm

Cassandra Project
   www.cassandraproject.org

Countryside Magazine (wells and water purification articles)
   www.countrysidemag.com

Environmental Protection Agency
   www.epa.gov/OGWDW/faq/emerg.html

Federal Emergency Management Agency
   www.fema.gov

Solar distillation
   www.epsea.org/stills.html
   www.permapak.net/solarstill.htm

Water-related links
   tjg.home.texas.net/water.html *(water treatment)*
   www.glitchproof.com/glitchproof/linabwat.html
   www.watertanks.com
   forums.cosmoaccess.net/forum/survival/prep/survival.htm
   www.y2ksurvive.com
   www.noahspantry.com/filter.htm *(water filter)*
   www.permapak.net *(water storage and purification)*

---

from complete, but it will give you a fairly good idea of just what is available. See how many are within 15 minutes of your home or apartment.

For safety's sake, water from any of these sources should be filtered and purified before being drunk!

Plumbing—There is water in your water lines even after the power goes out. To access it, turn on a faucet at the lowest point in the line (e.g., basement). If water doesn't flow out, also open the faucet at the highest point (e.g., upstairs bathroom). Water will then flow freely from the lowest faucet. Have a bucket at the ready!

Hot-Water Heater—Depending on size, some heaters contain as much as 40 gallons of water. However, because of heavy sedimentation, you should not drink or use this water.

Toilet Tanks—Tanks typically contain five to seven gallons of usable water. If, however, your tank has a commercial disinfectant (e.g., Tidy Bowl), you cannot use this water for drinking, even if you purify it! It can only be used for nondrinking purposes.

Water Bed—Here is an often overlooked supply of up to 400+ gallons of emergency water. You can use the water as is for nondrinking and noncooking purposes. However, to use your water bed as a drinking or cooking reservoir, you need to take the following steps: 1) Buy a new mattress and fill it with fresh water; 2) add two ounces of bleach for every 120 gallons of water (do *not* use algae inhibitor solutions!); 3) boil any water before using it. It is a good idea to empty and refill the bed at least once a year, and to test it with a water kit every three or four months for algae.

Swimming Pool—Since this is essentially a man-made pond, exposed to Mother Nature's elements, you should consider this to be a contaminated water source. Make sure that you boil it if you decide to use the water for drinking or cooking.

Rainwater—Set out bowls, pans, and buckets before it rains. Boil or chemically disinfect any water collected for drinking or cooking purposes.

Snow/Icicles—Consider all snow and icicles to be unclean. Do *not* eat them, since doing so will lower your core body temperature. Instead, melt and boil the frozen water.

Ice Cubes—Check out the ice cube trays in your freezer. If fresh, they can provide you with an immediate source of water, albeit a very limited supply.

Ponds, Rivers, et Cetera—You have to assume that any surface water is contaminated, no matter how clean it appears.

Use a bucket to collect the water, then filter and boil (or chemically disinfect) the water for drinking and cooking. You can use untreated water for nondrinking purposes, such as laundry, although filtering the water first is strongly recommended. You don't want to be pouring leeches into your underwear.

Spring—A spring is an underground water source that "leaks" through the earth's crust. Generally, a spring is drinkable if it is not contaminated by dead animal carcasses, chemical spills, et cetera. Until you are able to test the quality of spring water, consider it to be contaminated: filter and boil it before drinking.

Dew—Dew is a very reliable source of water. You can collect it as soon as it begins to form on grass until it finally evaporates in the morning sunlight. Collection is easy: Use a mop or an absorbent piece of cloth (e.g., chamois blanket, towel) and drag it through the vegetation. When saturated, wring it out into a bucket. Although this is a labor-intensive process, it works well. Just make certain that you boil or chemically disinfect it before drinking it; grass is teeming with bacteria and parasites. (*Warning: Do not collect and drink dew from grass or foliage that has been fertilized or treated with chemicals!*)

Indian Well—Dig a two-foot hole (12-inch diameter) in very moist soil—the wetter, the better. If done correctly, water will quickly seep into the hole. Wait for the suspended dirt particles to settle and then carefully dip out the clear water with a cup. The more you bail, the cleaner the water will become. Filter and purify the water before drinking it.

Water Still—Take a large clear plastic bag (a gallon-size Ziplok bag will do nicely) and fill it half-full with fresh, green leafy vegetation. Toss a small clean rock into the bag as well. Inflate the bag and tie it off (or, in this case, zip it shut). Carefully incline the bag on a table, bookcase, et cetera in bright sunlight such that the rock is positioned at the lowest point in the bag. The bag, now a miniature tropical jungle, will cause the water from the vegetation to evaporate. The moisture will condense on the inside of the bag, where it will dribble down and eventually gather at the rock. (Remember, the rock is at the lowest point!) Pour the water out and disinfect it before drinking.

There are a number of water-still designs that you can make using readily available materials. To learn more about these, refer to military survival manuals and to the Internet resources listed on page 63.

TIP **23** *Test your water for safety and quality.*

It is a good idea to test water six months or older with a chemical test kit before drinking it. If the water fails the test, then you have three options: 1) purify and use it; 2) use it for nondrinking purposes only; or 3) empty the container, sterilize it, and refill it with fresh water.

You can get water-quality test kits from a local hardware or plumbing store, a pool supply company, a garden center, or a mail-order company, such as Campmor and Major Surplus & Survival. They generally cost about $10 each for a chemical-contaminant test kit and a coliform-bacteria test kit.

TIP **24** *Rotate your water supply.*

Water, if bacteria free and stored properly, can have a shelf life of two years or longer. When opening containers, it is wise to follow the "first in, first out" adage. Hence, you would use water stored on April 11, 1999 (as indicated by the container's label), before water stored on September 27, 1999. By rotating your water supply, you are ensuring that your water remains as fresh as possible.

Food and Other Necessities

HAVE AN ADEQUATE AND SAFE SUPPLY ON HAND

When I think about an American family sitting down for a meal,
I cannot help but think about the tens of thousands
of people whose work went into producing that meal. . . .
I must confess, however, that until recently
I hadn't thought very much about the connection between
the food on our tables and computers.
—Dan Glickman, Secretary
U.S. Department of Agriculture

I am concerned that no one on this planet is assessing the potential negative impact of Y2K on the global food supply."

With that ominous statement, Ed Yardeni, chief economist at Deutsche Bank Securities, caused a group of senators he was testifying before to sit up and take notice. It was July 22, 1998, and the senators—all members of the Committee on Agriculture, Nutrition and Forestry—had gathered to discuss what Y2K could possibly do to America's agricultural base.

It didn't take long for them to learn the answer. Yardeni went on to say: "I suspect that the Y2K technological problem could significantly disrupt the food supply chain."

If our inventory and distribution systems collapse or if a prolonged blackout occurs, your local grocery stores could run out of food. If they do, what will happen? How bad will things get? It depends on how panicked people become and how willing they are to resort to violence to get what food they can find to stay alive.

Now, I want to be perfectly clear: I am *not* predicting that our country's food supply is going to—*poof!*—vanish into thin air. I am, however, saying that it is prudent and wise for you to have extra food on hand to deal with emergencies—Y2K or otherwise. This chapter shows you what issues to consider and, more specifically, what steps you need to take to establish a stockpile of food.

TIP 25 *Have an adequate supply of food on hand.*

How much food you decide to stash away for an emergency depends on 1) how much money you have and are willing to spend on buying supplies; 2) how much storage space you have available to you; and 3) your level of anxiety about Y2K. For some, an adequate food supply can be as little as three days of food; for others, a year's worth.

In the past, the American Red Cross recommended a three-day emergency food supply. However, now it is suggesting a week's supply in anticipation that Y2K could cause sporadic power outages and food distribution problems.

I recommend a 30-day reserve of nonperishable food, at the very minimum. If you have the means to do so, establish a six-month supply. Why? It is good insurance just in case you ever lose your job. It can take several months to go through the job search and interview process before you finally get hired. And, even then, you often have to wait two to four weeks before receiving your first paycheck.

By having six months of food on hand, you won't have to immediately worry about how you are going to put food on the table.

Before you rush out to the nearest grocery store, sit down and create a logical food-storage plan. This way, you will ensure that you and your family will have your basic nutritional requirements met.

For instance, the National Academy of Sciences recommends the following daily caloric intake values: 1600 calories for sedentary women and the elderly; 2200 calories for children, active women, sedentary men, and teenage girls; and 2800 calories for teenage boys, active men, and athletes.

Of course, a person's caloric intake varies according to genetics, level of physical activity, wellness, and metabolism. Try to create simple daily menus that take into account the following food items and servings:

Food Item	Servings (per person per day)
Bread, Cereal, Rice, and Pasta	6–11
Vegetables	3–5
Fruit	2–4
Milk	2–3 cups
Meat, Poultry, Fish, Dry Beans, Eggs, and Nuts	2–3
Fats, Oils, and Sweets	According to family practice

Serving size varies from category to category, as shown here:

Bread
   1 slice of bread; 1 oz. ready-to-eat cereal; or ½ cup of cooked cereal, rice, or pasta

Vegetable
   1 cup of raw, leafy vegetables; or ½ cup of cooked vegetables

Fruit
   1 medium size fruit; or ½ cup of chopped or canned fruit

Milk
   1 cup of milk or yogurt; 1.5 oz. of natural cheese; or 2 oz. processed cheese

Meats
   2–3 oz. cooked meat, poultry, or fish; 1 egg; ½ cup of beans; 2 tbsp. peanut butter; or 1 oz. lean meat

Fats
   According to family practice, but generally no more than 30% of your total caloric intake.

Since figuring out exactly what you need to buy can be an overwhelming task, try the following method. It is the simplest

way to define your emergency food stores. All you need to do
is get a large piece of paper and label it as follows:

	Breakfast	*Lunch*	*Dinner*
1			
2			
3			
4			
5			
6			
7			
8			
9			
10			

Now, fill in the chart with simple, easy-to-fix recipes while
striving for variety in food items. (Go ahead, blow off the dust
and thumb through your cookbooks! You can also refer to
Chart 5-1 for ideas.) This will leave you with 10 breakfast,
lunch, and dinner suggestions. Together, this represents an ongoing 10-day menu that you can repeat three times over a
month, nine times over three months, or for as long as you like.

All you have to do now is figure out exactly what foodstuffs,
spices, et cetera you need to buy, and in what quantity, to
prepare each meal for your family. (Remember, active teenag-
ers tend to eat more than lethargic parents! So be prepared to
buy extra food for certain meals.) Before buying these items,
make certain that each day's menu is nutritionally sound, calo-
riewise and vitaminwise. (In other words, 100 percent of the
recommended daily allowance of vitamins and nutrients, plus
the required calories.) You can determine this by looking at
the nutrition label printed on the cans and packaging. A glance
through your pantry and refrigerator, or a quick trip to the
store, will help you collect all the information you need.

Wasn't that simple? This logical approach to food buying
ensures a proper diet that provides you with a variety of foods.
Variety is extremely important, since people get tired of eating
the same food in a short period of time. (Who wants to eat
chili five days in a row?) And when they do—especially chil-

CHART 5-1

SAMPLE MENUS

Putting a menu together is not difficult. Use the following suggestions
to get your creative juices flowing. Then, pull out a cookbook and find
specific easy-to-prepare recipes that your family will enjoy, making certain to take into account any special dietary needs of a spouse or child
(e.g., low-salt diet, diabetes). When you have finished compiling a 10-day
menu, review it with everyone at a family meeting to make sure there
are no objections before you start purchasing supplies.

All of the following meals can be made from canned or prepackaged
foods, such as powdered eggs.

BREAKFAST

Oatmeal. Cereal. Omelette or scrambled eggs. Home-made bread. Jam
or jelly. Grits. Canned sausages. Pancakes. Hash. Dried Fruit.

LUNCH

Tuna fish. Canned chicken, chili, spaghetti, or ham. Soup. Vienna sausages. Peanut butter. Beef jerky. Macaroni and cheese. Stew.

DINNER

Canned ham, turkey, chicken, corned beef, Spam, shrimp, or salmon.
Rice mixtures. Couscous. Pasta salad (boil-in-bag). Spaghetti or pasta
with minced clams, shrimp, marinara sauce, cheese sauce, etc. Vegetables (canned or dehydrated peas, corn, or green beans). Beans and rice.
Macaroni and cheese. Mashed potatoes (real, canned, or flaked).

---

dren—they either start skipping meals or don't eat as much
food as they normally would. This can lead to malnutrition
and, subsequently, a host of related medical ailments. By following the suggested 10-day food rotation, no one will get
tired of eating a particular food. (They will be eating turkey
only three times a month, for example.)

When buying food, select items that require no refrigera-
tion, preparation, or cooking, and little or no water. Ready-to-

eat canned products (e.g., ham, fruit, tuna fish, turkey) meet these requirements. Also, try to select foods that are compact and lightweight, such as powdered milk, freeze-dried spices, and dehydrated fruits.

Additionally, be sure to add a few food treats to your stockpile. These are foods that make you feel good psychologically when depressed or ill, such as candy, cookies, or nuts. (Scientific research has shown that the act of eating causes your brain to release dopamine, a powerful chemical that makes you feel good.) So have each member of your family list three of his or her favorite foods—nutritionally good or bad, it doesn't matter—and then store away a small amount. When a difficult time strikes, pull it out. It will cheer everyone up.

Regardless of what you end up buying for your emergency food reserve, the most important rule is: *Buy and store what you eat!* In other words, don't stockpile anchovies if you can't stand anchovies. If you do, you'll have 20 cans in the basement for years to come. *Always* buy foods that you will enjoy eating. It will make your survival lifestyle much less stressful.

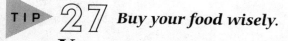

TIP 26 *Don't forget food for your pets!*

If you own any cats, dogs, gerbils, ferrets, et cetera you need to buy and stockpile, at a minimum, a month's worth of food for them. Although canned foods store best, you may not have a choice but to buy dried food. If so, store it in airtight containers. (See Tip 28.)

As cruel as it may sound, you should not share your personal daily rations with your pets. Why? You need your 2,000 calories to stay alive. If you begin scrimping on yourself, you could become malnourished and ill. Then who would take care of your pets?

TIP 27 *Buy your food wisely.*

You can do this once you have decided on your basic 10-day emergency food menu and you have written down a master shopping list of the items you need to purchase, do your shopping at a bulk discount store like Sam's Club. When you come across an item on your list, buy it and then stockpile it.

Do not buy large amounts of just a few items. I have occasionally seen people buy a six months' supply of flour, powdered milk, and pasta—and nothing else. They walk out of the store with just those three items. Granted, they can scratch them off their shopping list, but if the economy collapses in the next few days, guess what they are going to be living on? Right! Pasta, flour, and powdered milk!

A better strategy is to purchase smaller amounts of several items. Since your basic food menu is for 10 days, I suggest that you buy food items in 10-day quantities. As you fully complete a 10-day supply, begin stocking the next 10-day period, and so on, until you reach your final food-supply goal. For instance, if you intend to stockpile enough food for a month, then you will be shopping for three 10-day periods.

You may be tempted to forgo the planning process and all the shopping and, instead, rely on a mail-order company to mail you an adequate food supply. There are a number of companies that do this today, including AlpineAire, Major Surplus & Survival, Y2K Survive, and Perma-Pak. All you do is select how much food you want—three days, two weeks, one month, three months, six months, or one year—and then place an order. Within several weeks, a stack of prepackaged foods will arrive at your doorstep.

If you take this route, be prepared to empty your bank account. A year's supply of food for just one person can cost upward of $1,500. And that price usually doesn't include any real meat, just textured vegetable product (TVP) that is flavored to taste like beef and chicken. A three-month supply of the same food, but for two people, costs $800 or more.

By shopping around, you can find some excellent bargains. For example, Major Surplus & Survival sells a one-year food supply for one person—with real meat—for $995 (plus $130 shipping). It normally retails for $1,600. What does it contain? You receive 69 large cans filled with vegetables, rice, beans, et cetera plus 72 eight-ounce beef, chicken, and pork meals. All you have to do is heat and eat; there is no fancy cooking involved.

For those of you who have gourmet palates, you definitely will want to look at AlpineAire's Gourmet Reserves, which features delectable meals like chicken primavera, beef rotini, spaghetti marinara with mushrooms, and teriyaki turkey. A one-year supply for one person costs $2,899, plus $150 for shipping.

If you are tempted to buy your emergency food in bulk from a mail-order company, there are several things you need to consider and be aware of, including:

Storage—Buying food in bulk means you are going to be inundated with boxes. A one-year supply of food, for instance, can involve 25+ boxes, occupy 60 cubic feet or more, and weigh 600 to 1,200 pounds. Do you have adequate storage space? Can your home or apartment structurally deal with this added weight?

Calories—Not all meals are created equal. Before buying a large supply of food, ask the company how many calories they designed the meals to have. I have seen prepackaged foods range from as low as 715 calories per day to as high as 2,400 calories. Remember, your goal is to eat your minimum caloric amount daily.

Servings—The first thing you will notice when buying bulk prepackaged food is that it often comes shipped in airtight, moisture-proof No. 10 cans. These are large sturdy cans capable of storing 3.5 gallons. A single can typically contains a year's worth of just *one* food item—20 to 30 individual servings of corn, for instance. Problem is, once you open the can you will have to eat it all, otherwise it will spoil. You can avoid this problem if you can figure out a way to safely and effectively repackage the unused portion of food such as a vacuum sealer.

Expiration—Not every food-supply company marks the date when your food was processed and packaged. So you need to inquire how old the food is when you buy it. Age can adversely affect the nutritional value of the food.

Packaging—How the food is canned is important. If the

company is not vacuum- and nitrogen-packing their food, but relying only on an oxygen absorber, then they are not canning the food the best way possible. You need to know this before making a purchase.

Shipping—It is expensive to have bulk food (especially canned food items) shipped to your home. Most prices you see in catalogues do *not* include the freight costs.

Back Order—Most of the prepackaged food companies today are backlogged. Some are able to ship your order within a month, but many are not able to do so for three months or longer. So, if you want to buy these prepackaged foods, don't delay! Place your order ASAP, and make sure you get written confirmation that your order has been placed and when they expect to ship it to you.

Returns—Find out what the company's return policy is for damaged goods. When your shipment arrives, carefully inspect the cans and packages, looking for dents, cracks, bulges, and leakage. Bulging and leaking canned goods are unsafe to eat. Most companies require that you contact them before returning the damaged goods so they can get a claim number from the shipper (e.g., UPS). The shipper may or may not need to inspect the items and packaging, so hold on to all the original packing materials until you know for certain.

TIP 28 *Store your food properly.*

Like your emergency water supply, your food items must be properly stored away. Canned and dry-packaged foods generally store better—and longer—in cool, dark places. So once again, the basement makes an ideal storage space. Just make certain that it is dry: you don't want your food to become moldy or your flour to turn to paste. North-facing rooms, which tend to be cooler and darker than other rooms in the house, are good substitutes for a basement. Interior closets and half bathrooms (no hot, steamy showers!) are other possible spaces you can use.

Attics, garages, and sheds make poor storage facilities since they are often too hot, and harbor pests. The last thing you want to happen is to have mice and insects gorge themselves sick on your peanut butter or rice. (See Chapter 6 for more information about food safety issues.)

Unlike canned foods, dry bulk items like grain, beans, rice, and powdered products require special packing. Although many folks swear by metal cans (including the No. 10 can) for storage, they can be difficult to find locally. More often than not, you have to order them directly from the manufacturer. Some of the companies I am aware of are:

Eagle Can Company, Peabody, MA, 508-532-0400
Finger Lakes Packaging, Lyons, NY, 315-946-4826
American National Can Company, Chicago, IL,
    312-399-3000
United Can Company, Hayward, CA, 510-881-4531

An easier and oftentimes less expensive solution is to use plastic containers. You can purchase them from your local grocery, hardware, and retail store.

Always use new, clean, food-grade plastic containers. How do you know if it's food grade? There are two marks on the container that will reveal whether it is: look for the HDPE (high-density polyethylene) mark and the triangle-shaped recycle symbol with a "1" or "2" in its center.

Any container that you do end up buying should have a very tight-fitting lid to prevent moisture and air from leaking through and spoiling the food. You can place a food item directly into the container or, if you want to prevent it from developing a disagreeable plastic taste and odor, seal it first in a Mylar bag and then place it in the container. You can buy various size Mylar bags from a mail-order company like Major Surplus & Survival. They sell five bags, each measuring 20 by 30 inches, for $8.50. A storage-bag sealer, which you will need to seal the Mylar bag shut, costs $24.95.

All dry goods (e.g., cereal, rice, flour) need to remain dry, otherwise they will spoil or turn to goo if moisture seeps in.

To keep them dry, seal them in an airtight container or Mylar bag that also contains a desiccant pack. A desiccant is a mineral (e.g., silica gel) that absorbs moisture. A silica gel packet can be reused if you dry it in an oven at 250 degrees for several hours. (Note: Do not eat silica gel!)

To keep grains (e.g., wheat, barley, corn) and legumes (e.g., lentils, beans) fresh, seal them in an airtight container or Mylar bag and toss in an oxygen absorber. It is a chemical that literally removes oxygen from the air—to levels as low as 0.5

FOOD SHELF LIFE

You should always go by the expiration date stamped on the food item to determine its shelf life, but since many products use codes, you may not have a clue—mold aside—as to when it is time to throw something away. To decipher the expiration code, there are two things you can do. The first is to visit a Web site that reveals the code or shelf life, such as:

www.a1usa.net/gary/expire.html
www.waltonfeed.com/self/lid.html
www.ocweb.com/y2k/PFS.htm
www.glitchproof.com/glitchproof/storlifofgro.html

The second option is to call the manufacturer and ask for assistance. Their phone number is often printed on the food product label. Here are a few phone numbers of the more common food producers:

Del Monte	800-543-3090
Hormel	800-523-4635
Kraft Foods	800-543-5335
Libby's	888-884-7269
Lipton	800-328-7248
National Fruit Prod. Co.	800-551-5167
Pillsbury	800-328-6787
Planters	800-622-4726
Procter & Gamble	800-543-7276
Progresso	800-200-9377
Starkist	800-252-1587

percent—thereby retarding food spoilage and the loss of a food's nutritional value. Oxygen absorbers do *not* work in moist environments and should *not* be combined with a desiccant.

Where can you buy these two products? You can try a local hardware store or canning-supply store (e.g., Agway, Blue Seal). If they don't carry these products, you can order them directly from:

A & D Corporation of America, Los Angeles, CA,
   800-228-4124
IMPAK Corporation, Pasadena, CA, 818-398-7300
Multisorb Technologies, Buffalo, NY, 800-445-9890
Solvay Fluorides, Greenwich, CT, 800-842-9879

When storing your food supply in the basement, stack the items on a raised platform to avoid direct contact with the cement floor, which can become damp in rainy weather. (Metal cans *rust* when exposed to moisture.) Platform possibilities include wooden pallets, two-by-four studs, bookcases, wire shelving units, and metal storage cabinets.

It makes sense to group common foods together—store vegetables in one spot; meats in their own place; fruits and jams together in another. Doing so will make it easier for you to find items, and it will enable you to quickly see if you are running out of something.

As you add new items to your stockpile, use a permanent marker and write down in bold print the date you purchased the item. You should also circle the expiration date, which should be stamped somewhere on the packaging. (Not every food item is marked with an expiration date, so do the best you can.) Doing this will help you later on when you begin using your food to figure out which items to eat first. As with your water reserve, you will select foods on a "first in, first out" basis. (See Tip 31.)

TIP 29 *Prevent malnutrition from happening*.

Malnutrition will not be of concern to you if you plan nutritious, well-balanced meals for your emergency stockpile. However, because disasters and the survival lifestyle can be extremely stressful, your body's need for vitamins and minerals may increase.

Thus, you should take a multivitamin supplement daily. There are a number of brands on today's market that will suffice—Centrum, One-A-Day, and Thera Plus to name a few. Select one that meets your personal preference.

A word of warning: Give children a multivitamin that is formulated for their body mass and needs. Also, keep vitamin tablets containing iron out of your children's reach. If they accidentally eat too many of them—thinking that the tablets are candy—the iron could kill them.

TIP 30 *Eat perishable foods first.*

If Y2K or a natural disaster ever causes a blackout, do not haul out your emergency food supply. Instead, eat the foods found in your refrigerator. They are perishable, and if you don't eat them, they are simply going to spoil and be thrown away. By forcing yourself to empty the refrigerator—followed by the freezer and then, in turn, the kitchen cabinets—you are maximizing your resources and extending the life of your main food supply.

To minimize the number of times you open the freezer, post a list of its contents on the door. *This practice can keep the food frozen for up to three days.* By then, the power could be back on. If not, then you can visit your emergency food reserve.

TIP 31 *Rotate your food reserves.*

Earlier in this chapter, you were encouraged to buy and store what you eat. Now let's add something to it: *Eat what you buy.*

That is correct: you have to eat your emergency foods, even if there is no disaster. Why? Because food does not last forever . . . even if it is canned or nitrogen sealed. The longer food is stored, the more its nutritional value decreases. So too does its palatability. This is why nearly all food has an expiration or use-by date stamped on it somewhere.

At some point, six months from now or so, you should begin using the food in your stockpile. If you forget or refuse to do so, you may find yourself throwing everything away. If that happens, then this entire preparedness effort will have been a complete waste of your time, money, and effort.

When you begin to eat your emergency reserve, select and use food items with the oldest dates marked on them. (You did do this, didn't you?) As you take an item, replace it. That way your stockpile will never be depleted . . . and it will always be fresh.

TIP 32 *Don't talk about your food supply!*

This is important: No one outside your family needs to know that you are stockpiling food and other supplies for a possible emergency. If a disaster does occur and grocery stores in your area end up with bare shelves, starving people may resort to theft and violence to get food.

TIP 33 *Be self-sufficient: raise your own food*.

As has been mentioned, the purpose of an emergency stockpile is to buy you time to become self-sufficient. At some point—regardless of your preparations—you may run out of food and water, especially if there is a prolonged crisis.

Theft and bartering aside, there are only three major ways to get food: gardening, animal husbandry, and fishing/hunting. Each of these is time intensive, and none is guaranteed to work. For instance, you could try to grow crops (indoors or outdoors), but your efforts could fail for a number of reasons, including lack of fertilizer, a severe insect infestation, or drought.

Yet, in spite of all these odds, you *must* find food to survive. Discuss this issue with your family today so that together you can make plans as to what you will do in the future to put food on the table. Once you settle on a strategy, gather the information and equipment you will need to successfully implement it. It is also wise to undertake as soon as possible any specialized training that might benefit you (e.g., hunter safety, organic gardening, food-preservation methods, wild-plant identification).

TIP 34 *Have a backup stove for cooking.*

If you are without power for any length of time and you normally use an electric stove, then you will be unable to cook food. Fortunately, there are several alternatives you can choose from. The common drawback among all of them, however, is fuel availability. Sooner or later, depending on supplies and the distribution system, you will run out.

Woodstove—Many households in the northern United States heat with a woodstove since hardwood is plentiful and produces adequate BTUs when burned. For these folks, cooking will be no problem: they can place their pans right on top of the stove.

A new stove can cost from $900 to $2,000 depending on size, amenities (e.g., glass door), and BTU output. Also, note that you may have to add a chimney and/or flue, depending on your home's construction, which drives the final cost up even higher. (See Chapter 7 for more details.)

Camp Stove—There are a number of camp stoves on the market, varying in size, amenities, and BTU output (10,000 to 35,000 BTUs). Most operate on propane or white gas although occasionally you will find one that burns kerosene. You must use these stoves outdoors or inside a garage if it is raining (keep the garage door open!). You cannot operate a camp

---

CHECK IT OUT . . . YOURSELF

Food storage and safety information
  waltonfeed.com/grain/faqs
  www.redcross.org
  www.foodsafety.org
  www.fema.gov
  www.cassandraproject.org
  forums.cosmoaccess.net/forum/survival/prep/survival.htm
  www.fsis.usda.gov/OA/pubs/consumerpubs.htm

Food suppliers
  www.millenniumfoods.com
  scribble.com/y2k
  www.permapak.net
  www.arkinstitute.com
  www.y2kration.com
  www.y2ksupplies.com
  www.farmerdirect.com
  www.pridetv.com/survival/address.htm
  y2kfood.com/alpineair
  www.webleyweb.com/y2k/y2kfood.html

Stoves
  hearth.com
  chi.hearth.com/travis/travsearch.html
  www.permapak.net/volcano.htm

---

stove inside your home, even if you place it in a fireplace with
the flue open. That is because the stove creates toxic fumes
that can irritate the eyes and lungs, or cause you to pass out
and die.

The good thing about camp stoves is that they are affordable
($50 to $170), easily transportable, and take up little storage
space. You can also adjust the heat with a valve, meaning that
burned food will probably not be a problem. The major drawback of a camp stove is fuel storage: you can store only so
much fuel on your premises, be it white gas or propane. And

what you do store will be a fire hazard. So you need to be very, very careful.

A disposable propane cylinder (16.4 ounces) burns four and a half hours on low; one hour on high. That means you will need to stockpile a lot of fuel if you intend to cook three hot meals a day for your family. You can get around this problem somewhat, by buying a stove that is able to connect to a 20-pound (or larger) propane tank. But even then, you will eventually run out of fuel and have to refill the tanks—if propane is still available.

Outdoor Grill—These grills run on either charcoal or propane. In an emergency situation, they are useful in cooking foods, simmering soups, and boiling potatoes and pasta. Like camp stoves, the main drawback of an outdoor grill is fuel availability.

Candles and Warming Fuels—Cooking a meal over two or three burning candles is certainly possible, but it is not very practical. The same holds true for canned fuels like Sterno, which are used to keep fondue pots and chafing dishes warm. I consider all of these heating sources to be adequate for short-term emergencies *only*—one or two days max. And even then, they are only effective at warming a ready-to-eat meal.

Volcano—The Volcano is a conical-shaped outdoor stove that operates on charcoal briquettes or wood. The 18-pound steel stove is equipped with a very efficient draft system that allows temperature control. You can cook an entire meal using just 12 briquettes, which burn for two hours. In an emergency situation, 300 pounds of briquettes will last a family of six for a year.

You can get more information about the Volcano by reading Perma-Pak's fact sheet on the Internet at: www.permapak.net/volcano.htm

Solar Oven—Anything you can bake or boil in a normal electric or gas oven (up to about 400 degrees) you can cook in a solar oven. The actual baking time is dependent on three things: the quality of available sunlight; the type of food being cooked; and how often you have to refocus the oven's optical system.

One of the more popular brands on the market today is the Global Sun Oven (800-408-7919). It measures 19 by 19 inches and weighs only 21 pounds.

Campfire—While cooking over an open fire may conjure up romantic images of *Little House on the Prairie*, in reality, it is not always fun: smoke gets into your eyes and lungs, the heat singes your hair, flying embers land on your skin and clothes, and the soot is difficult to clean off pans (unless you soap the exterior first).

TIP 35 *Stockpile basic supplies*.

If you ask three friends what items you should stockpile for an emergency, you will get three different answers—most of it influenced by their own interests and perceived needs. The following list is no different, although it is as generic and as broad as possible.

Do not feel compelled that you absolutely, positively *must* have every single item listed here. Instead, use this list as a general guideline—a proverbial string around the finger to remind you not to overlook something.

Since you have done a thorough inventory of your home and personal belongings, you will find that you already have many of the following items on hand. That's good. Compare your inventory against this list and check off any items you have.

General Supplies

cooking supplies
    pots and pans
    aluminum foil
    plastic wrap

wax paper
Ziplok bags (various sizes)
paper plates
paper cups

plastic utensils
spices
utensils (e.g., spoons, spatula, kitchen knives, can opener)
backup stove and fuel
storage containers
medicine dropper
kitchen towels
food thermometer
canning equipment
grain mill
Mylar bag sealer
desiccants and oxygen absorbers
cooking oils
water jugs
gardening seeds
steel wool
pot holder mitts
aprons
rubber gloves
water filter/purifier

lighting
candles
flashlights (battery or solar powered)
batteries
lamps (oil, kerosene)
lantern (propane, white gas)
matches (strike-anywhere, waterproof)
spare parts for lamps and flashlights
Cyalume light sticks

alternate heating source (e.g., woodstove)
generator

fuel (e.g., gasoline, propane, kerosene)
CB radio
battery-operated smoke alarm
battery-operated carbon monoxide alarm
battery-operated radio
games, books, and entertainment items
clothesline and clothespins
pencil sharpener
pins (straight, safety)
sleeping bag
emergency "space" blanket
wool blankets
chemical heating pads
cash
fire extinguisher
signal flare and whistle
compass
medical supplies (see Chapter 7)
sewing supplies
needle and thread
excess fabric
thimble
scissors
personal
eyeglasses
medications
makeup
clothes (adequate supply for all seasons)
winter jacket
sturdy boots
rain gear

thermal underwear
hats
gloves (work, winter)
insect repellent
sunglasses
firearm(s) and ammunition
fishing equipment
hunting knife
pocketknife
binoculars
sunscreen
pens/pencils
Chap Stick
lotions
contraception (condoms, birth
control pills, foam)
pregnancy test kit
extra shoestrings
backpack
vitamins
tools
rope (minimum: 100 feet, $\frac{3}{8}$ inch
thick)

twine
wrenches
hammer and nails
screwdrivers
oil/grease/lubricants
duct tape/masking tape
pliers
saws
degreasing solutions
gardening tools
shovels
ax/hatchet
honing stone
metal files
wheelbarrow
sledgehammer
wire
plastic tarps
firearm cleaning kit and
materials
solar-powered battery charger
extra Ni-Cad batteries
fire starter

Sanitation Supplies

toilet paper
towelettes
bar soap
toothpicks
nail files/clippers
tissue
sponges
baking soda
laundry detergent
washtub

buckets
broom
solar shower bag
rubbing alcohol
liquid dish soap
combs/brushes
cotton balls and swabs
feminine hygiene
tampons/sanitary pads
douche

underarm deodorant
baby supplies
  diapers
  ointments
  bottles/nipples
  sterilizing equipment
  baby wipes
  breast pump
contact lens solution and
  cleaning products
dental floss
mouthwash
toothbrush and toothpaste
denture cleaning products

disinfectant (e.g., ammonia,
  alcohol, hydrogen
  peroxide)
pesticide
bleach (5.25 percent sodium
  hypochlorite solution)
room deodorizers
garbage bags (various sizes)
portable toilet
steel-wool scrubbing pads
paper towels
razors
shampoo

Pets

food (canned and dry)
toys
vitamins
medications (e.g., heartworm,
  thyroid)

litter
shampoo
bedding
flea powder

TIP 36 *Stockpile items for bartering purposes.*

If the world turns upside down as a result of Y2K, then you may be well served by having a stockpile of extra items that you can trade for services or things you cannot provide yourself.

Coffee—Nearly everyone starts the day off with a steaming hot cup of joe. Because of this, coffee will always retain its value. You can buy ground coffee by the can, or buy whole beans by the bag. If you opt for the beans, realize that folks will need access to a grinder. This may limit the number of potential buyers for the beans, thereby decreasing their value.

Tools—Consider stockpiling a variety of quality handtools (e.g., saws, screwdrivers, wrenches, hammers, planes); someone will need them to build something or to make a repair to a generator, car, et cetera.

Fuel—Propane, natural gas, and kerosene will be in great demand for use in heaters and stoves, as will wood and charcoal briquettes. Gasoline will be needed for cars, chain saws, and small engines. Remember to treat gasoline with a stabilizing additive (e.g., Sta-Bil) before storing, otherwise it will gum up within a few months. You also need to keep the gasoline free of water.

Alcohol—People drink when times are bad. Hence, all hard liquors—whiskey, vodka, bourbon, gin—will trade well. So will many wines. Beer, however, will not since it does not have a long life expectancy and becomes flat tasting within a year.

Tobacco—I can personally attest to the purchasing power of tobacco: when I was visiting Morocco as a teenager, I traded packs of my mother's cigarettes for beautiful handwoven clothing and other goods. If you decide to stockpile tobacco, I recommend cigarettes, cigars, or chewing tobacco.

Ammunition—Without ammo a handgun, rifle, or shotgun is simply a useless assembly of metal parts. Demand for ammunition could increase if people rely on firearms for hunting and self-defense. If you decide to stockpile ammunition for rifles and handguns, acquire the common calibers: 9-mm, .45ACP, .22LR, .38, .223, .308, .30–30, or .30–06. For shotguns, consider 12-gauge rounds, especially buckshot and rifled slugs, since they are used for hunting large game. Also, consider stockpiling cleaning and repair parts for firearms.

Essential Spare Parts—An essential part is something that a person needs in order to make another item operate properly. For instance, without batteries or a good bulb, a flashlight will not work. Examples of so-called backups include springs, bolts, screws, lightbulbs, electrical wiring, firing pin, knife sharpener, rubber bands, ammo, lighter, shoelaces, duct tape, butane/propane canisters, and batteries of all shapes and sizes.

Knives—Collect a small stash of knives for bartering purposes: pocketknives, hunting knives, survival knives, fighting knives. Keep several sharpening stones and ceramic sharpening rods on hand, too. A dull knife is a butter knife.

Incidentals—These are items that most people need or use on a regular basis but will run out of if the nation's distribution system collapses. Examples include: matches, salt, toilet paper, razors, makeup, diapers, toothpaste/toothbrush, sugar, dental floss, contact lens solution, underarm deodorant, feminine hygiene products, shampoo, soap, and condoms.

Health and Sanitation

Quit worrying about your health. It'll go away.
—Robert Orben

Today we live in a society where we take sanitation and hygiene for granted. With a flick of a switch we wash our dishes, grind up our garbage, and flush away waste. We luxuriate in half-hour showers, pamper our skin with lotions, and get rid of body odors with specially formulated powders and gels. EMTs are a phone call away, diseases are controlled with the pop of a pill, and the food supply is constantly monitored for contamination.

All of this will dramatically change, however, if Y2K causes an extended blackout or distribution problem. Without electricity, hot showers and dishwashers will be a thing of the past. Without a functioning distribution system, store shelves will go bare and households will run out of dish soap, disinfectants, toothpaste, and dozens of personal hygiene products.

If you fail to take action now, you could be setting yourself up for a disaster. Why do I say that? Because it has been proven—ever since the 1347 appearance of the deadly Black Death in Europe—that poor sanitation and hygiene breed disease. This fact is well-known to public-health professionals, who routinely deal with the aftermath of floods, earthquakes, and man-made disasters.

TIP   ③⑦ *Prevent illness through good hygiene and sanitation practices.*

The human body is absolutely filthy. This is a truth that most people conveniently forget. The body gets dirty from a number of sources, including sweat, cutaneous organisms, airborne particles, and direct contact with soil.

Because we are such dirty creatures, it is imperative that we follow good personal hygienic practices. Doing so reduces our likelihood of becoming ill. Simple hand washing, for instance, gets rid of many disease-causing organisms that we come into contact with.

Hence, it is important that you do not scrimp on bathing and hand washing. Always wash your hands with soap and clean water after handling foods, soiled items, and untreated water (e.g., lake water). Likewise, wash them before eating, and after using the toilet and diapering the baby. How long should you wash your hands? The rule of thumb is to vigorously scrub your palms and fingers for the length of time it takes you to slowly sing one verse of "Happy Birthday."

Do not bite your fingernails no matter how stressful things might be or put dirty fingers in your mouth. (Soiled fingers contain much more than dirt!) Likewise, don't pick scabs; keep them covered to prevent infection.

As for bathing, you should try to shower daily. If there is no power, you can take a so-called solar shower. A solar shower is a dark-colored rubber bag that absorbs enough of the sun's energy to heat five gallons of water to as high as 130 degrees. Such devices are widely available from camping/outdoor stores and mail-order catalogues. To use, simply hang a full bag in a sunny spot for several hours. When the water is warm enough for you, take the bag inside and hang it from your shower head and proceed from there.

HOME-MADE CLEANING PRODUCTS

If there is a distribution problem as a result of Y2K, you may run out of your commercial cleaning products. Fortunately, there are a number of home-made cleaners you can mix yourself:

Flea and tick repellent
Scatter pine needles, fennel, rue, pennyroyal, or rosemary on your pet's bed or blanket. Feed your pet brewer's yeast, vitamin B, or garlic tablets.

Multipurpose cleaner
Mix ½ cup of ammonia, ⅓ cup of vinegar, and ¼ cup of baking soda in a gallon of warm water.

Air freshener
Simmer cloves and cinnamon in boiling water.
Leave an open box of baking soda in the room.
Set out a dish of vinegar.

Drain opener
Use a plunger or mechanical snake.
Pour ½ cup of washing soda into the drain, then pour two cups of boiling water into the drain. Flush the drain weekly with boiling water.

Laundry presoak
Make a paste of washing soda and water. Apply to dirty spots.

Metal cleaner
Make a paste of salt, vinegar, and flour. First, take ¼ cup of salt and add enough vinegar to dissolve it. Then add flour to create a *damp* paste. Rub paste on metal and polish with soft cloth.

Source: NH Department of Environmental Services' Household Hazardous Waste Program

---

If you don't own a solar shower, then bathe in the rain (not a thunderstorm!) or use a stove to heat some water in a bucket and then use soap and a washcloth to clean your body, paying close attention to the feet, armpits, crotch, hands, and hair since these are prime areas for infestation and infection.

If water is scarce and your choice is to either shower or have water to drink, then save the water. (Remember, you need drinking water to survive!) Instead of bathing with water, remove as much of your clothing as practical and expose your body to the air and the sun's rays for an hour. Be careful not to get a sunburn! Exposure to the sun's ultraviolet rays kills much of the bacteria on your skin.

Good personal hygiene also means getting adequate rest and sleep. You need to learn to make yourself comfortable under less than ideal conditions to maintain your sanity. Stress is known to weaken the immune system, thus making you more susceptible to illness.

If you have a daughter who is nearing the age of her first menstruation, then make certain you stockpile extra sanitary napkins and tampons for her use. (Don't forget your own supply!) Many families overlook this aspect when preparing for an emergency. Also, make sure that you have an adequate supply of general feminine hygiene products, such as douches, yeast infection ointments, and lubricants.

Other hygienic products that you should consider having available—for everyone, male and female—include medicated body powder, jock itch spray, athlete's foot ointments, mouthwash, and underarm deodorant. For a more complete list, see Tip 35 in Chapter 5.

As for sanitation issues, keep your food preparation area as clean as possible. Use bleach to kill any bacteria that might be present on the counter or cutting board. Be ever alert to cross-contamination of foods and avoid it. In other words, do not use a knife that has come into contact with raw chicken to slice up vegetables. Use a utensil once, and only for one purpose. Then thoroughly wash it.

Dispose of kitchen waste properly. (See Tip 40.) If possible, all biodegradable waste should be collected and used to create a compost pile in your backyard. The resulting dirt can be used to enrich gardens. (It is also a good source of worms that can be used as bait for fishing.) If composting is out of the question, then place the kitchen waste in a garbage bag and properly dispose of it.

When washing your pans, plates, utensils, and silverware, carefully use dish soap and steaming hot water. Do *not* use untreated water to wash dishes! (FYI: A half-and-half mixture of dish soap and vinegar makes a nice antibacterial solution that not only cleans but softens your hands.) If you use a sponge or dishcloth, sterilize it once a week in boiling water for 10 minutes; it is a breeding haven for potentially dangerous diseases.

To reduce your water needs for dishwashing, use paper plates.

And last, if you have young children, disinfect their toys using a solution of one cup of bleach in five gallons of warm water. Either soak the toy in the solution or use a cloth dipped in the solution to thoroughly clean the toy.

T I P ❸❽ *Prevent food from spoiling*.

Having food on hand for an emergency is one thing, but keeping it is another. Why? Quite simply, you are not the only one who wants the food—so do insects, bacteria, mold, and rodents. Hence, you are going to find yourself conducting daily combat with infestation and microscopic organisms.

Fortunately, there are two weapons that you can use to win this fight—temperature and storage.

Bacteria love warm weather. When food, cooked or raw, is allowed to reach and remain at ambient temperature for several hours, the bacteria throw a party. So do molds. They multiply and quickly take over the food. If you eat any of this food, you may become ill.

The trick to defeating these "bugs" is to observe this rule: *Keep cold foods cold, and hot foods hot*. Nearly every foodborne-disease outbreak that I was involved with while I was at the Health Department for eight years was the result of someone ignoring this simple rule. Thousands of people suffered needlessly because of it.

To be safe, do what most health professionals do: *assume that all food is contaminated*. This holds true about 90 percent

FOOD SANITATION TIPS

- Cook fresh poultry, fish, ground meats, and variety meats within two days; other beef, veal, lamb, or pork within three to five days.
- Keep raw meat, poultry, fish, and their juices away from other foods.
- Wash your hands before and after handling any raw food item.
- Sanitize the counter or cutting board often using a bleach solution (one teaspoon of chlorine bleach in one quart of water).
- Use cooked leftovers within four days.
- The following foods should keep at room temperature for a few days. Still, discard anything that turns moldy or has an unusual or disagreeable odor:

  Butter or margarine
  Hard and processed cheese
  Fresh fruits and vegetables
  Dried fruits and coconut
  Fresh juices
  Fresh herbs and spices
  Fruit pies, breads, rolls, and muffins
  Cakes (except cream-cheese frosted or cream filled)
  Open jars of vinegar-based salad dressings, jelly, relish, taco sauce, barbecue sauce, mustard, ketchup, olives, and peanut butter.

Source: U.S. Department of Agriculture's Food Safety and Inspection Service

of the time, especially with regard to meats, seafood, and poultry products. Thus, make certain that you keep cold foods cold—use dry ice, chemical ice packs, or snow—and hot foods hot. In fact, cook or heat your meals to at least 160 degrees to kill any organism that may be present. A chef's meat thermometer will help you determine the temperature. Simply stick the thermometer into the thickest portion of the meat without it touching any bones.

As for leftovers, do not allow them to sit out on the counter for more than an hour after serving the meal. (Note: Throw away any cooked, unrefrigerated food if it has been left out on the counter for two hours or more, regardless of what it looks like.) Wrap the leftover food in plastic wrap or foil and place it inside a picnic cooler filled with dry ice, ice cubes, or chemical ice packs. If you have a large amount of a particular leftover—say, for instance, a gallon of soup—then pour it into several small and shallow containers and place them in the cooler. Doing this cools the food more quickly, thereby preventing bacteria from growing.

If you do not have a cooler, then improvise. People have been known to use wooden boxes, fishing tackle boxes, Styrofoam containers, and thick plastic bags. In fact, one person dug a pit three feet into the ground. He lined it with blocks of ice and placed his foods in this primitive "au naturel" icebox.

The second weapon in your fight against food spoilage is to *safely store your foods,* including the items that make up your emergency food stockpile. In Chapter 5 you were told to store dry food items like flour and cereal in airtight containers, along with silica gel packets, in a dark, cool location. There was a reason for this: bacteria and mold need sufficient moisture, warmth, and a food supply to live. The silica gel removes the moisture, the containers keep out insects and rodents, and the 40- to 60-degree environment somewhat retards growth. Thus, foods last longer.

As for so-called wet-pack foods—items that are either moist (e.g., ham) or canned with a liquid (e.g., vegetables, spaghetti)—storage requirements are similar. Keep the cans in a dark, dry place. This is because heat spoils food more quickly and moisture causes the cans to rust, thereby increasing the risk of leakage and contamination.

Although you may think you don't have to worry about canned foods spoiling, the consequences to your health and well-being are actually greater if a canned food does go bad. In both home- and commercially canned foods, *if the can is bulging, leaking, smells bad, or spurts out liquid when you open it, throw it away!* It has been improperly packaged and may contain botulism, a dangerous toxin that can kill you if eaten. Thus, you need to be alert and carefully inspect all canned goods *before* opening them.

TIP 39 **Control insect and rodent infestations.**

The presence of any pest—most notably mice and rats—should alarm you. First, they are eating *your* food, the food that you struggled so hard to find, buy, and stockpile. And second, mice and rats are vectors of many diseases, including Lyme, rabies, hantavirus, and plague. So you need to take action at the first sign of a chew mark or dropping. Better yet, be proactive and rodent-proof your food supply.

How? First, make sure your food supply is safely packaged. (See Tip 28.) Second, keep your storage area spotlessly clean and free of debris. Third, remove things the rodents might use for shelter, such as boxes, junk, and protected enclosures. Fourth, dry up sources of water. Fifth, routinely inspect your stockpile for leaking cans or packages. If you find one, remove it and throw it away.

And last, strategically place some talcum powder in areas that mice and rats will travel through, leaving telltale marks behind. This is your trip-wire warning that you have visitors. Generally, mice and rats travel along the walls, so put a powder patch on each wall in the emergency food storage area. Also, place some powder near entry points, such as doorways and cracks in the foundation. Remember, rats can squeeze through cracks a half-inch wide.

If, in spite of these efforts, your home does become infested with rodents, then you have to use more violent steps to get rid of them.

Trapping—The traditional spring-loaded snap trap is quite effective. Place several along the walls and bait each with whole nuts, bacon squares, or peanut butter. Small wads of cotton work well, too—they look for nesting material.

Glue Boards—These are super sticky pads measuring about three by five inches that you place in infested areas. When a curious mouse or rat investigates, it is "superglued" to the pad and unable to run. If you decide to use these, do not place them in dusty or wet conditions—they impair the trap's effectiveness.

Poison—Premixed poison baits are commonly found in hardware stores. Although there are three types of poisoning methods used, I recommend the anticoagulant baits. All you do is place the bait in strategic areas and then wait. The mice and rats will take pieces of the bait back to their nest and eat it; several days later they are dead. On the plus side, if your pet or child accidentally eats some of the bait, there is an antidote: vitamin K. (Confirm this with the package's medical treatment directions.)

Weapon—If you live in a rural area where it is legal to own and fire a weapon, you may find it feasible to kill rodents, especially rats, with either a .177 pellet gun or a .22 rifle. Be very careful if you use this method—a .22LR bullet can travel in excess of a mile.

Predators—Don't rely on cats or dogs to control your rodent infestation. In general, they do a poor job. Instead, if you live in a rural environment, consider raising and using nonpoisonous snakes, such as rat snakes, king snakes, and black racers. When set free to roam your property, they feast on rodents.

Regardless of how you kill rodents, wear rubber or latex gloves when removing them from the premises for disposal or burial. That's because they may harbor a disease like hantavirus or ticks that are infected with the bacteria that causes Lyme disease.

Now, I don't know about you, but I happen to like mice and snakes. What gives me the heebie-jeebies, though, are insects, especially those multilegged ones that I find sharing my food. I can clearly recall several instances in my life of finding weevils doing the backstroke in my cereal bowl, and of ants skittering across my ham-and-cheese sandwich. I still get goose bumps about it, even though I know weevils and ants are not dangerous.

Insect infestations occur in a variety of foods, including flour, pastas, dried fruits and vegetables, grains, beans, legumes, jerky, sugars, and pet foods. When buying any food item, examine it closely, looking for adult insects or larval eggs. If it is clean, store it in an airtight, moisture-proof container so that it cannot be infected later on.

If you have a dry food item (e.g., grains, flour) that is infected, use a colander to sift the larger-size bugs out. Then treat the remainder by placing it in a freezer at 0 degrees for at least three days. If this is not possible, then consider adding diatomaceous earth (DE) to the product.

And what is that? Diatomaceous earth is fine dust made from the fossilized skeletons of ancient aquatic plants. The dust particles are extremely sharp—on the microscopic level, that is. When DE is added to grains and seeds, it scratches the insects' outer protective waxy exoskeleton. This, in turn, disrupts the insects' internal water balance. Within a short period of time, the insects die from dehydration. The infestation is over.

This procedure is widely used today by commercial food processors. Most of us eat diatomaceous earth on an almost daily basis without even realizing it. The dust does no damage to the food, it is edible by humans, and it is a mineral that our bodies can digest. You can purchase DE from a number of sources, including canning-supply stores and natural food stores. If they do not carry it, then order it directly from one of these companies. Specify that you want to buy *food-grade* DE!

All Gone!, Vero Beach, FL, 800-373-3423
Fossil Shell Supply Co., Amarillo, TX, 800-370-9920
Eagle-Picher Minerals, Reno, NV 800-663-5517

If you purchase diatomaceous earth to prevent insect infestation, one pound ($5) protects about 300 pounds of grain. A one-time application (follow directions on package) lasts up to 10 years and keeps dry products smelling fresh. When mixing DE in with your flour, grains, and seeds, *avoid inhaling the dust!* The abrasive dust can cause problems to your lungs. This also means you need to keep curious children away from your bucket of DE as well. It is safe to eat, but not to inhale.

TIP 40 *Do not allow garbage to accumulate.*

Y2K could slow or halt the collection and disposal of garbage if there is a power outage (trash compactors use electricity) or a fuel distribution problem (garbage trucks need gas). If you live in an urban environment, this will create some problems. Rotting garbage not only smells terrible, it attracts rodents, insects, and stray/wild animals. It also serves as a breeding ground for disease.

One common method is to burn and bury all rubbish that has no useful purpose; cans are flattened first. The ashes are then placed in a four-foot-deep trash pit, and a thin layer of either lime or soil is raked over it. When the pit is full, it is capped with a thick, four- to six-inch layer of soil, and another trash pit is dug. This burn-and-bury method stops the garbage from attracting flies and significantly reduces any foul-smelling odors.

Never dispose of hazardous waste—gasoline, oil, paint, thinner—in this manner. Instead, recycle or donate what you can, and dispose of the rest in accordance with your city or town's regulations.

TIP 41 *Dispose of human waste properly.*

For most of us, using a toilet will not be a problem, even if Y2K triggers a power outage. As long as you have access to water, all you have to do is manually fill the toilet tank with three to five gallons of water and then flush. Gravity takes over from there.

Problems arise when the sewer system itself fails—many rely on electric pumps to move sewage through the piping. If this happens, you may have to use the emergency shut-off valve to prevent the sewage from backing up and spilling into your bathroom. *Then* you will be without a toilet.

Fortunately, you have several options available to you. First, you can purchase a portable toilet. Examples include:

Bucket Toilet—A 14-inch-tall bucket with a snap-on hinged seat and cover. Disposable plastic liners are inserted into the bucket. It usually has a 200-pound weight limit. Prices range from $25 to $35.

Folding Toilet—An X-shape design with a snap-on seat. Disposable plastic liners attach to the frame. It usually has a 200-pound weight limit. Price range from $10 to $20.

Fresh-Water Toilet—A two-piece toilet that has a 2.5- to 3-gallon fresh-water-holding tank and an equal-capacity holding tank. A chemical deodorant is added to the water to minimize odors. The toilet usually has a 250-pound weight limit. Price range from $50 to $110, depending on amenities.

Your second option is build your own latrine. If you go this route, you can build either a traditional outhouse or a military-style trench pit.

Regardless of what you end up building, there are three things about latrines you need to remember: 1) Locate the latrine far enough away to ensure privacy, but not so far away that people are reluctant to hike out there to use it. 2) Never defecate or urinate in or near your water supply! 3) Use a disinfectant spray to keep the latrine as clean and inviting as possible.

Outhouse—Dig a four-foot-deep hole and build a toilet seat over it. For privacy, you can either build an actual structure or string up a shower curtain around it. After using, sprinkle a thin layer of soil or wood ashes over the waste to reduce odor and prevent flies from swarming. (Note: Lime and disinfectants kill the bacteria that decompose human waste.) You should also add some natural enzyme (e.g., Bio-Green Digester) to help decompose the feces. If possible, place a cover over the latrine opening. Just remember to remove it before using!

Trench—This is a very simple toilet that requires you to dig a trench measuring four feet long, one foot wide, and two to three feet deep. To use, you simply place a foot on either side of the trench and squat. Use the excavated earth (or wood ash) to cover the feces. Once the trench is full, cover it and dig another trench parallel to it. For privacy, you can hang a blanket or shower curtain around the trench.

Soak Pit—This makeshift urinal is made by digging a two-foot hole and filling it three-quarters with pebbles and stones, and then capping it with dirt. A large plastic funnel (available at hardware stores) is shoved into the pit. Although this construction works well for both men and women, consider having two available—one for each sex. To make things more comfortable, a folding camp toilet with a plastic liner can be placed directly over the soak pit. Simply cut a small hole in the bottom corner of the liner and direct it into the funnel.

TIP 42 *Have a well-equipped first-aid kit.*

The list of potential medical emergencies is long. The three things standing between an injury and death are time, skill, and supplies. The faster you are able to respond, with the proper supplies and correct medical knowledge, the more likely you will be able to save the patient's life.

Thus, you need to have a well-stocked first-aid kit. You can either buy a complete first-aid kit from a store or mail-order company, or purchase the items yourself, one by one, from a local pharmacy. The latter is usually a more expensive proposition, unless you are simply supplementing an existing first-aid kit.

Prepackaged kits are priced according to their contents. You can expect to pay anywhere from $25 to $80 for a fairly complete first-aid kit.

The following list of medical items is divided into two categories. The first is of basic items that all first-aid kits should have. The second is a list of optional items that will make your first-aid kit more comprehensive; pick and choose depending on your finances and medical treatment capabilities.

Regardless of what items you buy, look for quality and cleanliness. As for disinfectants and ointments, pay attention to their expiration dates, which are stamped on the product itself. Store all first-aid items in a clean, waterproof container, which itself should be kept in a dry and easily accessible location. Check the kit's contents once or twice a year for leaks and damage, and to replace any expired products.

Bare Minimum, Basic First-aid Kit

first-aid book (*Note: Read it* now *or take a first-aid course. You won't have time to refer to a book when an emergency occurs!*)

latex gloves (two pairs minimum)

antiseptic towelettes (e.g., benzalkonium chloride)

hydrogen peroxide

sterile wound-closure strips (e.g., Steri-Strips)

butterfly bandages

Band-Aids (assorted sizes)

gauze pads, small (two-, three- and four-inch)

gauze pads, large (18- and 24-inch)

gauze rolls (two- and three-inch)

sterile eye pads

knuckle bandages

triangular bandages

five by nine bandage

two by three moleskin patch

gauze tape (one inch by 30 feet)

adhesive tape (one inch by 10 feet)

elastic Ace bandages (two-inch and three-inch widths)

tourniquet

antibiotic ointment (e.g., Neosporin)

lubricating jelly (e.g., K-Y jelly, Vaseline)

tongue depressors, wooden (Note: Can also be used for splinting.)

sunscreen
surgical soap
bandage scissors
acetaminophen (e.g., Tylenol)
ibuprofen (e.g., Advil)
tweezers
needle
safety pins (assorted sizes)
pencil and paper
syrup of ipecac
activated charcoal

Optional Medical Items

ammonia inhalants (smelling salts)
instant cold packs or compresses
calamine lotion
surgical suture kit
waterproof matches
alcohol prep pads
dehydration tablets (electrolyte tablets)
hydrocortisone creme (1 percent solution)
thermometer
povidone-iodine swabs
emergency blanket (metallic foil)
Bloodstopper trauma dressings
wound probe
snake-bite kit
Kelly forceps
hemostat forceps (designed to stop blood flow from a vein)
instant heat packs
Kiss-of-Life rescue mask
oral airway set
nasal airway set
eye irrigation solution
eye drops (e.g., Visine)
cervical collar
stethoscope

blood pressure cuff
air splint (inflatable)
sterile scalpels
single edged razors
penlight
burn ointment
mirrors
wire mesh splints
teething gel (for babies)
antidiarrhea medicine (e.g., Pepto-Bismol)
antacids (for stomach upset)
mineral oil
bed pan
fingernail clippers
dental emergency kit
ear drops
pocketknife (multiblade)
medicine dropper
laxative
douche
enema kit
magnifying glass
arm sling
cough drops
allergy medicines
diaper rash cream
children's Tylenol
Pedialyte (electrolyte fluid for children)
glucose
insect repellent

Remember to anticipate the medical needs of your family: stockpile extra supplies of medically required medications that they will need, such as insulin, nitroglycerin, diuretics, blood pressure prescriptions, antidepressants, Epipens, asthma and allergy drugs, and hormone replacement medications.

Take care to properly store all prescriptions! Many drugs require storage at a specific temperature and humidity, otherwise their effectiveness is significantly decreased. Discuss with your pharmacist or physician the storage limitations for any medication you intend to stockpile.

TIP 43 ***Know how to handle basic medical emergencies.***

You never know where you will be or what you will be doing when a medical emergency arises. For this reason you should receive some training in first aid. Many community colleges, hospitals, Red Cross chapters, YMCAs, and local health organizations offer basic and advanced courses in first aid, CPR, and rescue. Sign up for the next class; the skills you learn could save your life or the life of someone you love.

If you already have some training in first aid, then now is an excellent time to review your manuals and, if time permits, take a refresher course to hone your skills. Remember, in many life-threatening situations, you won't have time to review a handbook. Your actions have to be prompt and correct, right from the start.

Here are some of the unique Y2K-related medical conditions you may encounter. Undergo training to learn how to handle them.

Cold-Weather Injuries—The millennium bug will strike in the middle of winter, when the weather is miserably cold. If the power goes out for an extended period of time, you and others are going to become cold if you do not have adequate winter clothes or an alternate heating source, such as a woodstove. Hence, hypothermia is likely to set in. You need to be able to recognize the symptoms of this deadly condition and know how to quickly stop it. The same holds true for frostbite and trench foot.

Hot-Weather Injuries—If Y2K sporadically disrupts the power supply and distribution system throughout 2000, then you may find yourself some summer day baking in 100-degree,

---

CHECK IT OUT . . . YOURSELF

Hygiene information
    www.foodsafety.org/dh/dh049.htm

Refrigerators
    www.lehmans.com
    www.realgoods.com

First aid
    www.fema.gov/library.htm
    www.redcross.org
    www.nsc.org

Food safety
    www.usda.gov/fsis

Drug prescriptions and information
    www.y2kdoc.com
    www.bonners-ferry.com/y2kmeds

Medical devices
    www.fda.gov
    www.medical-devices.gov.uk
    www.shef.ac.uk/uni/projects/hij/y2kdef2.htm
    www.fda.gov/cdrh *(radiological devices)*

---

90 percent humidity weather without an air conditioner. In miserable weather like this, your body cannot cool down as it should, and it will overheat, literally frying your brain cells. Hence, you need to be trained and equipped to treat heat exhaustion, heat stroke, sunburn, and dehydration.

Carbon Monoxide—This is a very dangerous gas since it is odorless, tasteless, and invisible. Carbon monoxide is produced as a by-product of burning fuels, such as propane, kerosene, gasoline, coal, firewood, and oil. If you heat or power (e.g., with a generator) your home in an emergency with any of these fuels and do not adequately ventilate the rooms, you may pass out and even die. (After the ice storm of January 1998 hit New England and Canada, thousands of people ended up in emergency rooms as a result of inhaling carbon monoxide from their indoor heaters.)

Animal Bites—As mentioned earlier, animals are attracted to garbage. So the chance of human-animal encounters will increase the longer trash pickup is delayed. Since animal bites can be nasty—animals violently shake their head side to side after biting—it is imperative that you know how to stop serious arterial bleeding. This includes bites to the neck, a common target of larger animals, such as dogs. As for rodents, you will need to know how to treat bite injuries to the fingers, face, and limbs of children. And last, you should have a working knowledge of rabies since it can be carried by any unvaccinated warmblooded animal, domestic or wild.

TIP 44 *Get copies of your medical records.*

This only makes sense. You do not know who will be treating you for medical ailments in the future. If you have to go to a hospital emergency room, the physicians there may not be able to access your file electronically if Y2K has crept into the system. It is much better (and safer!) to have a copy of your medical history, including immunizations, medications you have taken, laboratory tests, surgical procedures, allergies, and general health information (e.g., heart rate, blood pressure, weight). Besides, gathering this information now will allow you to review the accuracy and completeness of your records. If you do come across a discrepancy, have it fixed immediately!

TIP 45 *Get important medical/dental treatment done before 2000.*

Overall, the majority of hospitals and America's health care system are far behind in their preparations for Y2K. Too far behind, in fact, to catch up: according to a U.S. Senate report, 64 percent of hospitals have no plans to test their Y2K fixes and some 90 percent of doctors' offices are unaware of their susceptibility to Y2K problems.

One of the more dangerous Y2K catastrophes-in-waiting involves Medicare. Administered by the Health Care Financing Administration (HCFA), Medicare has over 100 mission-critical systems—yet only seven at this time are year 2000 compliant. If HCFA does not improve its efforts, Medicare *will fail.* Thus, the ability to provide payments for benefits and services will be jeopardized.

Making matters worse, hospital records could get messed up by Y2K glitches, medical equipment could fail, medical supplies could run out, and prescriptions could go unfilled.

It is truly a disaster waiting to happen.

For these reasons, consider postponing any elective surgery between December 1999 and February 2000. *Elective surgery* refers to procedures that are not required to keep you alive and well, such as a face lift or liposuction. There is no sense in taking an unnecessary risk until you see how Y2K actually affects the health-care system.

One last thing to do before December 1999 is to make sure you and your children are current with your immunizations. The tetanus vaccine is especially important since the organism is found in dirt. If the year 2000 finds us all trying to survive by living off the land, the tetanus shot will keep you from getting tetanus if you cut yourself.

TIP 46 *Check to see if your medical device is Y2K safe.*

If you require a medical device to maintain your health, you *must* find out if it is Y2K safe since many medical devices and diagnostic equipment use computer technology to function. According to the Food and Drug Administration (FDA), this includes pacemakers, defibrillators, auto-injector systems, ventilators, insulin pumps, dialysis machines, life-support equipment, and heart monitors.

How do you find out if your medical device is safe? There are three ways: 1) ask your physician; 2) call the manufacturer directly; or 3) use the Internet to visit the FDA's Med Watch (www.fda.gov/medwatch/what.htm) or Federal Y2K Biomedical Equipment Clearinghouse Database (www.fda.gov/cdrh/yr2000/y2kintro.html). What is the difference between these two Web sites? Well, the Clearinghouse provides specific information regarding Y2K's known or suspected impact on medical devices, while Med Watch posts warnings about a wide variety of problems involving drugs, biologics, medical devices, radiation-emitting devices, and special nutritional products (e.g., infant formula or dietary supplements).

If you call the manufacturer and ask about their product's Y2K status, make sure that you get their reassurance *in writing!* Many firms are quick to say, "The product is fine, don't worry," to avoid panicking the public. When you ask the company to put it writing, they know that their response is legally binding and, thus, they are more likely to be honest in their assessment.

The reluctance of companies to disclose their product's Y2K status is illustrated by the FDA's frustrating efforts to learn this information as well. According to the General Accounting Office, there are nearly 100,000 medical devices on the market today. Since January 1998, the FDA has been trying to get Y2K compliance information on these devices, but has not received much cooperation from the manufacturers. Out of 16,000 requests for information on product compliance, the FDA has received only 1,975 replies.

Power, Light, Heat, and Other Vital Matters

CREATURE COMFORTS ARE IMPORTANT TO YOUR WELL-BEING

I believe that Y2K will be equivalent to throwing a million monkey wrenches into the "engine" of the global economy, and that it will lead to a depression similar in severity and duration to the Great Depression.
—Ed Yourden,
Computer Consultant and Y2K Expert

The Department of Transportation is moving toward January 1 at a snail's pace, with only 53 percent of its systems year 2000 compliant. . . . The FAA's antiquated air traffic control system is a significant part of the problem. Its progress rate makes the horse and buggy look like rapid transit.
—Congressman Stephen Horn (R-CA)
February 22, 1999

A person can just as easily drown in three inches of water as in 30 feet of water. This observation readily applies to Y2K: it doesn't matter how mild the situation seems, it will still be a disruption to our lives.

Don't think so? Then ask the 1.2 million residents of Auckland, New Zealand's largest city. On February 20, 1998, the downtown section of Auckland was plunged into darkness when the last of Mercury Energy's four 110,000-volt power cables failed. For the next month and a half, 8,000 businesses and 5,000 people who lived downtown were without bank machines, cash registers, burglar alarms, gasoline pumps, lights, and air conditioning. Food rotted in refrigerators, trash piled up in buildings, and clouds of choking fumes from generators settled over the city.

As the days dragged on and turned into weeks, people began to lose their jobs as companies, one after another, were forced to shut their doors. Downtown businesses collectively lost $60 million a week. Those who did work often did so in stifling 90-degree buildings whose windows could not be opened. One practical switchboard operator stripped to his underwear to endure the heat while answering calls.

Simply put, the conditions were atrocious. Said Deputy Prime Minister Winston Peters, "We've got one of the most modern cities in the world being reduced to Third World status."

And all because just *four* power cables went belly-up. How is *that* for your proverbial three inches of water to drown in?

This incident occurred nearly two years before the arrival of January 1, 2000. If three inches can convert a large city like Auckland into a Third World environment, just imagine what the 30-foot wave of Y2K will do to our world.

At this point in the book, two of the most important issues regarding emergency preparedness have been addressed— water and food. Now it is time to look at other important things you must contemplate and make decisions about. Fair warning, though: as you read through this chapter, you will feel each separate issue tugging at your consciousness, begging you to give it top priority. Given time, you may feel over-whelmed—as if you are drowning in your own three inches of water. That is natural. Do not panic. More important, do not throw your arms up in exasperation and turn your back on your Y2K preparations. As Auckland demonstrates, you must push ahead and prepare for the flood. There is no easy way through this.

T I P **47** *Consider having an alternate power source.*

Fortunately, there are many options available to pro-vide electricity. Granted, you will not have the same power available to you from these devices as you normally do, but with careful planning you will have enough to run key appliances.

Before searching for a power resource, sit down and determine which items in your home or apartment you want to run when the power is off. Furnace? Refrigerator? Hot water heater? Oven? Stovetop? Hair drier? Every electrical appliance requires a certain amount of electricity. For instance, a space heater needs about 1,300 watts to operate; a refrigerator, 1,000 watts; a single electric stove burner, 1,500 watts.

You need to identify the most "wattage-hungry" appliance as well as the total wattage of all the items you want to operate simultaneously. Once you have done this—and added an additional 500 to 1,000 watts for the appliance's initial start-up—then you know how powerful your power source must be and what you need to look for when shopping. Just remember, though, the more power you want, the more it will cost.

Generator—There are three kinds of generators: gasoline, propane, and diesel. Of these, gasoline generators are the cheapest, and propane generators are the cleanest (and don't smell). However, diesel engines outlast gasoline generators by twice as long and are more fuel efficient. They also pose less of a fire hazard than propane. Because of this, most people end up buying a diesel generator (3,500 to 6,500 watts), even though they cost a bit more.

There are two ways a generator can be used. First, you can plug an appliance directly into the generator. Since generators usually have a limited number of outlets built in, you can operate only so many appliances at once. Another drawback is that since the generator is outdoors, how will you get the electricity indoors to run, let's say, the refrigerator? Are you willing to have extension cords snaking all over your home?

The second and more popular option is to have an electrician wire your electrical panel so that you plug your generator into it when the power goes out. (This is known as a cut-over box.) You simply tell the electrician which household appliances you want the generator's electricity to power and he makes the necessary connections. This method means no extension cords are needed. When you want to operate a designated appliance, you just turn it on.

Warning: For safety reasons, when you connect your generator to the house, you must disconnect your house from the power grid. Failure to do so may injure or kill a line repairman working nearby on the electrical lines. Call your local electric company for advice on how to safely handle the disconnection.

When shopping for a generator, consider the following:

1. What is its *continuous* duty rating? In other words, how much power can it generate over a sustained period of time?
2. How much power does each outlet on the generator have? For instance, a generator may produce a total of 5,000 watts, but it may only send 1,000 watts to each of three outlets and 2,000 watts to the fourth outlet.
2. How do you start the generator? Does it need a battery or does it work off a pull start?
3. How long will a tank of fuel last? This will give you an idea of how much fuel you will need to stockpile.
4. Is the generator air cooled or water cooled? Air-cooled generators are light and less expensive than water-cooled engines.
5. What is the generator's oil needs? Ask if the generator has full-pressure lubrication. If so, it means the generator has an oil filter and it requires fewer oil changes than a generator that has so-called splash lubrication.
6. Does the generator have an auto-shutdown feature to protect the engine from damage if the oil runs low?
7. How clean is the electricity produced by the generator? This is important if you want to run a computer or other voltage-sensitive equipment off the generator. Such devices need electricity that does not fluctuate very much.

There are a number of portable generators on today's market. Brands you are likely to encounter include: Coleman Powermate, Dyna-Winco, Fischer Panda, Generac, Gillette

Gen-Pro, Kohler Power Systems, Lister Petter, MagneTek, and Yamaha. Many of these manufacturers have Web sites on the Internet. An index page can be found at: 209.52.183.182/agitator/Generator/generator_manufacturer_links.htm

Anticipate spending a *minimum* of $1,000 for a quality 5,000-watt generator; $1,600 for a 6,000-watt generator. This expense is why many people chain generators to something to prevent theft when they are pulled out of the garage and used. In disaster situations, a generator is worth its weight in gold.

Power Inverter—This is a device that plugs into your car lighter and allows you to use the car battery to power small devices, such as a laptop computer, coffee maker, small TV, or battery charger. You can usually find them in retail stores (e.g., Circuit City, Radio Shack); they sell for about $100.

Batteries—You can purchase large deep-cycle batteries similar to those used in golf carts (6 volt, 220Ah) to operate low-wattage appliances. To do so, you will need an inverter to convert the battery's direct current (DC) into alternating current (AC), which appliances use. To recharge a drained battery, use either a generator or solar panels.

If you go this route, buy a large battery bank. The bigger the bank, the more the electricity storage, the less recharging that needs to be done, and the longer the life. A decent deep-cycle battery costs $75 to $220, weighs 65 to 120 pounds, and has a life expectancy of three years or more.

Note that batteries used in recreational vehicles and boats are *not* deep-cycle batteries. They are a hybrid between a true deep-cycle battery and a shallow-cycle battery. They will serve well in a pinch, but not for long. They have a life expectancy of only 18 months or so.

Wind and Water—Both wind and water require devices that capture and transform their power into electricity that is either stored in batteries or sent directly into the home as direct current (or, with an inverter, as alternating current).

For wind power, you need a steady breeze in excess of nine mph. Hence, place the turbine high off the ground, since wind is usually smoother and faster at greater altitude. For the windmill to reach its rated power of 500 to 1,500 watts, the wind must blow at least 25 mph.

As for water power, the turbines are built to handle high-pressure, low-volume water. In other words, if you can get the water to *drop* quite a distance—regardless of how little water actually falls—you will be able to generate electricity. So if you live on the banks of the Mississippi River, which has tremendous volume of water but no vertical drop, you will not be able to generate much power.

Hence, you must live near a stream or river that you can manipulate to create a vertical drop of at least 20 feet. This drop does not have to happen in only one place. People often use piping to move the water over the land to a lower point, thereby creating the power produced by a natural waterfall. Most microhydro turbines are designed to handle a maximum water flow of 200 gallons per minute.

The problem with both windmill and water power is the fact that they create direct current instead of alternating current. Direct current does not travel well over wire and is not used by household appliances. Therefore, if your home is more than 500 feet away from the turbine, you need an inverter to transmit the power.

Solar Power—Although expensive (every 100 watts of solar power costs $600 to $750 in panels) solar power is a strong alternative power source. Why? Because the sun, in some form, brightens our day for 8 to 14 hours. That is a tremendous amount of free energy that we can tap into.

How does solar power work? The solar panels (aka photovoltaic array) collect the sunlight—10:00 A.M. to 3:00 P.M. is the peak period for collection—and convert it to direct current, which is then stored in batteries. When power is needed, a $1,000 inverter converts the stored DC into AC.

Many homeowners combine solar power with a generator to provide a long-term power solution. A 5,000- to 7,500-watt generator can serve as a backup when there is a sunlight shortfall or when there is a sudden, increased demand for energy (e.g., guests, deep-well pumping, washing machine).

The main drawback to solar power is its initial expense. After that, it becomes increasingly cost efficient. In fact, over the long term, solar energy beats out generators.

TIP ▶ **48** *Choose an emergency heating system.*

There are several choices to choose from:

Woodstove—This is a good option if you have access to seasoned firewood and have adequate space to stack the wood. Depending on where you live and what your home's insulative properties are, you can burn through three to ten cords of wood a year.

Before you buy a woodstove, ask yourself two questions: How much heat do you want it to provide? (In other words, are you looking to heat one room or the entire house?) And where do you intend to install it?

Your answer to the first question determines the size and heat output (which is measured in BTUs) of the stove. And your answer to the second question determines whether you will get a free-standing stove or a fireplace insert.

In light of Y2K, there is a third question you might want to ask: Do you want to be able to cook on your woodstove? If so, then the fireplace insert is probably out of the equation.

There are essentially two types of woodstoves: "cats" and "noncats." Both burn off wood gases to reduce waste and improve heat output, but they use different methods. Cats have a catalytic converter that burns off smoke through a long, slow, controlled-combustion process, while noncats recirculate the smoke and reburn it in a second chamber.

Of the two, you will find that noncats have smaller fireboxes than cats. This means you will have to use shorter logs. It also means more trips to the woodpile to refuel the stove.

To figure out what size woodstove you should buy, measure the dimensions of the rooms you want to heat, keeping in mind that woodstoves do a better job warming large, open

PREVENTING CARBON MONOXIDE POISONING

Carbon monoxide is a colorless, odorless gas that is produced by the incomplete burning of fuel from a space heater, woodstove, fireplace, et cetera. Common symptoms of carbon monoxide poisoning include nausea, headache, disorientation, dizziness, and fatigue. Very high levels can cause death.

Here are some tips to keep your household safe from this invisible Grim Reaper:

- Open flues when fireplace is in use.
- Use proper fuel in kerosene space heaters.
- Do not use ovens and gas ranges to heat your home.
- Make sure your furnace has adequate intake of outside air.
- Do not use unvented gas or kerosene heaters in enclosed spaces.
- Do not burn charcoal inside your home, RV, or cabin.
- Make sure that the stove or heater is vented to the outdoors and that its exhaust system does not leak.
- Inspect and clean your heating systems, chimneys, and flues each year.

The National Center for Environmental Health has a checklist you can use to prevent carbon monoxide poisoning in the home, car, or RV. You can access it on the Internet at: www.cdc.gov/nceh/programs/heeh/monoxide/cocklst.htm

Sources: National Safety Council and the Centers for Disease Control and Prevention

areas than a maze of smaller rooms. Once you have the measurements, then visit HearthNet on the Internet and use their BTU calculator: hearth.com/calc/btucalc.html

By plugging in the numbers, you will quickly have an answer as to how many BTUs per hour it will take to heat those rooms. For instance, a room that measures 36 by 24 feet needs between 10,368 and 20,736 BTUs per hour depending on insulation and the climate.

What are the drawbacks to using a woodstove? First, if you do not have an existing chimney, you will have to have one installed to vent the smoke and gases. That means greater expenses. The same holds true for a hearth: if you do not have acceptable flooring, a cement or stone hearth will have to be installed. Again, this means more out-of-pocket expenses.

Second, woodstove heat is dry heat, which can cause skin irritation. (To alleviate this, keep a pot of water simmering on the woodstove to add moisture to the air.)

Third, you need to learn how to build and maintain a *good* hot fire. It takes work to keep a fire going for all your heating needs. If, for instance, you do not get up at midnight to stoke the fire, you will awake to a cold house.

Fourth, if you have children, a hot woodstove poses a hazard. Children must be taught not to touch or play with the stove.

And last, depending on the model you buy, a woodstove can be quite expensive. Prices range from $800 to $2,500. You then have to add the price of installation on top of that, plus the cost of seasoned firewood.

Some of the more common woodstove brands are Avalon, Vermont Castings, Jotul, Lopi, and Napoleon.

Gas Stove—Gas stoves look very similar in style and design to woodstoves. There are two types of gas stoves: vented and vent free. In the vented category, there are two stove designs: top vented (i.e., the vent goes through the roof) and direct vented (i.e., the vent goes through the wall). If you have an existing chimney or if your home is a single story, you will want to look at top-vented gas stoves. They sell for $600 to $2,000 plus installation costs.

If your home does not have a chimney or if it is two stories or taller, a direct-vented stove will serve you better. A hole is punched through the wall behind the stove and the vent is then installed. Direct-vent stoves sell for $1,000 to $2,000 plus installation costs.

As for vent-free gas stoves, they require no chimney at all since the burning process is so clean and thorough (99.9 percent), there are no residues. Virtually all the gas is converted to heat. The only by-products are water vapor and carbon dioxide. For safety purposes, vent-free stoves are equipped with an oxygen-detection safety pilot (ODS). It measures the oxygen level, which is normally about 20 percent. If for some reason it drops below 18 percent, the stove immediately shuts off. So you don't have to worry about dying in your sleep.

More than 7 million homes in America alone use vent-free gas stoves. This is because the stoves are easy to install, they require no electricity, they operate on either propane or natural gas, they humidify the home when turned on, they do not produce any soot or ashes that need to be disposed of, and they are inexpensive to purchase (a 30,000-BTU unit typically sells for less than $400 and is capable of heating 1,500 square feet).

If you are interested in finding a vendor that sells vent-free gas heaters visit the Gas Appliance Manufacturers' Association's Web site and search their list of members. Their Internet address is: www.gamanet.org/consumer/ventfree

Note that vent-free gas burners have been approved for use in 43 states—California, Massachusetts, and New York being the notable exceptions. (Canada prohibits their use as well.) Both California and New York, however, are presently in the process of approving vent-free stoves.

Warning: Commercial gas-operated space heaters, unless specified otherwise, are not to be used indoors in a closed environment! These heaters are often used on construction sites to speed the drying and curing of wet cement and paint. The same is true of heating devices that attach directly to a 20-pound propane tank. These items need to be operated in a well-ventilated area.

Pellet Stove—A pellet stove resembles a woodstove except that it burns small pellets made from compressed wood waste. Since these stoves rely on microprocessors to determine how much fuel should be burned, and since electricity is needed to operate the forced-air system to distribute the heat to the room, pellet stoves are *not* a viable emergency heating solution for Y2K concerns.

Masonry Stove—A masonry stove is a monstrous stove weighing more than two tons. It burns wood, but at a very high temperature (2,000 degrees) for a short period of time (two hours). The heat radiates from the stove for several hours, heating the home.

By using a masonry stove, you only have to tend to it twice a day in cold weather. It burns 20 to 30 pounds of wood split down to three-inch diameters during each burn. The high temperature nearly eliminates creosote problems.

Masonry stoves are also known as Swedish stoves, and come in several designs with various features (e.g., oven, range, corner units). Although they are powerful, they are expensive: prices begin at $4,000. For this reason, it may not be the best solution for you. For more details, contact the Masonry Heater Association of North America (703-620-3171).

Kerosene Heater—You can purchase these at hardware stores (e.g., Home Depot) and other retail stores, such as Sam's Club and Fingerhut. They come in various sizes, operate on kerosene fuel, produce adequate heat (5,000 to 25,000 BTUs) and are fairly inexpensive ($150 to $250). A single one-gallon tank of kerosene will burn for 9 to 10 hours.

The drawbacks to using a kerosene heater include: 1) kerosene smells and some people become ill or get headaches; 2) you will need a supply of wicks to keep the heater going for any length of time; and 3) the heater, unless specified otherwise, must be used in a well-ventilated area to avoid carbon monoxide poisoning.

Coal Stove—Coal comes in several grades of quality, the best being anthracite (aka hard coal). This dense fuel burns extremely hot with no visible smoke or creosote. A ton of anthracite costs $100 to $150 and can produce as much or more BTUs than a cord of wood.

There are several drawbacks to using a coal stove. First, coal produces 10 times more ash than a wood fire. So be prepared to safely dispose of it.

Second, you must clean the coal stove, smoke pipe, and chimney immediately following the burning season in the spring since this sulfur-based ash becomes corrosive when mixed with moisture. Stainless-steel chimneys are especially at risk of being damaged by the acidic ash. To neutralize the acid, some chimney sweeps pour baking soda in to the chimney. (Note: Do not mix the ash in with your garden dirt. It will acidify the soil to excess and kill your plants.)

Third, coal can be difficult to ignite and burn. It takes a lot of patience and practice to learn this skill. (See hearth.com/what/coalstoves.html for tips.)

And last, as with woodstoves, coal stoves are not cheap. Depending on the brand and amenities, a good coal stove can run $1,000 to $2,500 plus installation costs.

TIP 49 *Find ways to keep warm.*

To ward off the cold, have adequate and appropriate winter clothing. This should include ski wear, wool shirts/pants (wool will keep you warm, even if wet), mittens, caps, wool socks, scarves, thermal underwear, and waterproof, insulated boots.

Always dress in layers to trap warm air, and make certain that the layer directly next to your skin is not made of cotton. If cotton becomes damp from your sweat, it will only chill you. Instead, wear silk thermal underwear. The moisture will pass through to outer layers, where it belongs.

If you do any strenuous physical activity, remove the outer layers of clothes to avoid sweating. When you stop, put the layers back on.

In addition to clothing, consider buying a sleeping bag to keep you warm. There are a number of brands and styles to choose from. Goose-down mummy bags are extremely warm (and expensive!), but if the feathers get wet they are useless. For this reason—or if you are allergic to down—look at Hollofil II or Quallofil insulated sleeping bags. These man-made fibers are constructed to trap more air for greater warmth. Sleeping bags of this type cost between $99 and $149. A variety of mail-order companies sell them, including REI, L.L. Bean, Campmor, and Cabela's.

Regardless of what kind of sleeping bag you buy, make sure that you take the following points into consideration:

Temperature Rating—This indicates the coldest temperature at which the bag will keep you comfortable. (Notice, I did *not* say warm!) If you live in the northern U.S., go for the maximum rating of −20 or −30. If you live in the central U.S., a rating of 0 to +10 should be fine. And, if you live in the balmy South, select something with a +10 to +20 rating. Note that even if the rating is −30 degrees, you can still feel cold depending on your circulatory system, clothing, and body temperature. Sleeping bags work best if you wear as little as possible. Damp undergarments can keep you chilled, regardless of your sleeping bag's temperature rating.

Size and Shape—Sleeping bags come in different sizes and shapes. Make sure yours will comfortably fit your body frame. (Extrawide bags are available.)

Chest Tube and Hood—Examine the opening of the sleeping bag to see if it has a special collar to trap the warm air inside. This will keep your shoulders and upper chest/back warm. Your sleeping bag should also have a hood (with a drawstring). This allows you to enclose everything but your face inside the bag, thereby minimizing heat loss.

TIP 50 *Winterize your home or apartment.*

The term *winterize* means to improve your home's insulative properties so that it stays warm longer, and is not severely subjected to Mother Nature's elements. People who live in northern climes are accustomed to winterizing their homes every fall.

Here are a few suggestions that will reduce heat loss and physical damage to your home during winter months:

- Check windows and doors for drafts. (Hold a lit match or cigarette lighter next to the cracks. If the flame flickers, you have a draft.) Add insulation strips—felt or rubber—to doorjambs to reduce drafts. Stuff towels under doors not in use to prevent air flow. Caulk windows if they are drafty.

- Hang window quilts over large windows to reduce heat loss. Hanging thermal-lined curtains works well, too. (Also, consider stretching plastic-seal film over a window.)
- Wrap insulation around pipes, especially those found exposed in the basement, under an outdoor porch, or running along outer walls.
- Close your chimney flue when the fireplace or woodstove is not in use to prevent cold air from entering the house.

TIP 51 *Choose a light to see by at night*.

From both a practical and psychological standpoint, it makes sense to have emergency lighting. It not only allows you to extend your day into the evening, but it relieves anxiety (this is especially important where children are concerned), and makes your home feel more safe, warm, and cozy.

There are a number of options where lighting is concerned, which means you are likely to find something that will meet your needs at a cost you can afford. Just be aware of the carbon monoxide danger, and use the following products in well-ventilated areas. (See "Preventing Carbon Monoxide Poisoning" on page 118.)

Candles—The nice thing about candles is that they are generally long burning (a finger-size candle made from beeswax burns an inch an hour), smokeless, and come in different fragrances, which helps freshen a room. The major danger from candles is that they represent a fire hazard. Therefore, you need to place candles in a safe spot.

Buy both emergency candles and large pillar-style candles. Emergency candles are made from dense, nontoxic, slow-burning wax. How slow? A 2-inch-diameter, 4.75-inch-tall candle can burn for up to 50 hours! Nuwick makes canned candles that burn for 44 hours ($8) and 120 hours ($13). If you need more light or heat, or if you need to heat something, simply add another wick to the can.

Oil Lamps—An oil lamp casts quite a bit of light (60 to 75 watts), depending on its construction and type of oil used. Just remember to buy extra wicks and several bottles of oil or liquid paraffin to last you awhile. It is also a good idea to buy an extra glass chimney or two, just in case the original breaks.

Although there are many brands of oil lamps on the market, the Aladdin lamps are touted by users as the best and brightest. The glass-base, 20-inch-tall Aladdin Genie 11 sells for about $55, and the metal-base, 18-inch-tall Watchman B-165 goes for about $65.

Drawbacks to oil lamps include the obvious fire danger, and smoke/soot from too much wick being burned. Also, if you drop a glass-base oil lamp, it may shatter. (If the lamp is lit at the time, you could end up with a huge fire as the oil spews around the room.)

Kerosene Lamps—These lamps are similar in design to oil lamps, but do not put out as much light (40 watts). Another drawback is that kerosene has a strong and disagreeable odor. People who have asthma or other respiratory problems usually have problems with burning kerosene.

Lanterns—These camping-style lamps burn propane, butane, or white gas, which causes one or more cloth mantles in the lantern to glow, thereby illuminating the immediate area with 200 watts of bright light. You can adjust the light level by turning the gas-control knob.

Coleman is perhaps the best-known lantern maker. Their products range from the $40 two-mantle propane lantern (burns 16.4-ounce bottles) to the $70 Powerhouse gas lantern. The former burns 16.4-ounce propane bottles (18 hours on low, 7 hours at high), and the latter uses white gas (14 hours on low using just two pints). Of the two, the Powerhouse puts out 40 percent more light and its operational cost is 1/3 that of the propane lantern.

If you purchase a lantern, buy extra mantles (they need replacing when the cloth sack eventually rips). Make sure you operate it in a well-ventilated area to avoid carbon monoxide poisoning, and that children do not touch its hot metal surface.

Cyalume—Cyalume is a flexible plastic stick that you snap in half and shake. When the stick's two internal chemicals interact, a bright glow is given off—white or colored, depending on the stick casing. Cyalume light sticks are ideal for emergency situations, such as marking a path in the woods, a stairwell, or a broken-down car. Children find them reassuring in the middle of a storm or in the dark of the night. A six-inch-long stick glows for 8 to 12 hours, and costs as little as $1.50 if bought in quantity.

Flashlights—Flashlights are a poor choice for long-term lighting needs. They are only useful when portable lighting is required (e.g., searching the outside of your home at night), or when you need to see something in a tight or dark area (e.g., replacing an electrical fuse in the basement, cleaning the bore of a gun). The drawback to flashlights is that the life expectancy of their batteries is short. A two-battery D-cell flashlight, for instance, lasts only seven to eight hours when used intermittently. Kerosene, however, burns for 27 hours on one 31-ounce filling.

There are, however, self-powered and solar-powered flashlights available. The Dynamo flashlight ($10) has you repeatedly squeezing the grip to generate electricity, while the solar-powered flashlight from Patrick Technologies ($15 to $20) relies on stored solar energy to cast a beam.

Regardless of what kind of flashlight you use, make sure that you have extra bulbs on hand and, if applicable, a good supply of batteries. If you want to save on the cost of batteries, consider buying rechargeable Ni-Cad batteries. They can be recharged by a solar recharger as long as you have sunlight available to you. A double-A battery takes about three to four hours to fully recharge.

TIP 52 *Find a way to stay in touch with the world.*

If the telecommunications system is messed up as a result of a Y2K glitch, then you may be without a phone for several days while telecom workers try to get things working again. This scenario could recur several times in 2000 and beyond, as key spike dates come and go.

(Note: One thing you may want to avoid is being on the phone December 31, 1999, as the rollover occurs. It is possible that you will receive a bill for making a 100-year phone call! How much will that cost? In excess of $7 million!)

To stay informed on the local level as to what is happening, use a citizens band radio. Popular in the early 1980s, there are now more than 50 million CB units in use in America. With it, you can chat with people up to 150 miles away, although 10 to 20 miles is more typical, depending on local geography and atmospheric conditions. There are three types of CBs: mobile, base station, and handheld. I suggest using the mobile version simply because it runs off your car battery via the lighter instead of batteries. Mobile CBs are inexpensive, costing about $50 to $75 for a 40-channel model (although top-of-the-line models run $150 to $400).

If the 911 system collapses as a result of Y2K, you could still use your CB radio to call for emergency medical or police assistance on Channel 9. This channel is generally monitored by police and REACT—Radio Emergency Associated Citizens Teams. (Don't think your 911 system could go dead? Think again! New York City's 911 system crashed for an hour on Sunday, January 30, 1999, leaving hundreds of emergency calls unanswered. The crash allegedly occurred as a result of a Y2K test being done.)

To keep in touch with family members, consider using two-way radios. They generally give you a two- to five-mile range, which allows you to monitor the whereabouts of your children, spouse, or even a hunting buddy. Motorola's TalkAbout 250 Plus radio runs $110 per unit, and its TalkAbout Distance DPS costs $205 per unit.

If you are interested in finding out what is going on in the world (How is the rest of the world surviving Y2K? Has war broken out?), then I recommend the BayGen radio. This radio uses a Baylis generator instead of batteries. You simply wind the crank for 20 seconds or so and get a half hour of listening.

The BayGen Freeplay FPR1 costs about $99 and covers AM (520–1700), FM (88–108 MHz), and shortwave (3,000–12,000 kHz). The nonshortwave version—the FPR-2—costs $80, but I encourage you to spend the additional $20 to get the shortwave. Why? If widespread power outages occur in the U.S., then most of the news and information will be coming from independent radio operators around the world.

In fact, the U.S. military and federal government rely on this network for emergency communications. It is known as MARS—Military Affiliate Radio System—and it was established in 1948. MARS was used in the aftermath of the 1989 San Francisco earthquake.

If you do buy the Freeplay FPR1, then buy the *World Radio TV Handbook* ($24.95). It lists the schedules, frequencies, and addresses of shortwave broadcast stations around the world.

TIP 53 *Be aware of the potential travel risks.*

You have probably heard frightening stories about planes falling out of the sky and trains colliding head-on as a result of a Y2K glitch. How realistic is this threat? In a phrase: it's not. *But* that does not mean there will not be any problems at all.

The FAA itself has acknowledged that it was late in getting started on Y2K remediation efforts—they didn't create a Y2K program office until February 4, 1998. Although the agency has been working hard to catch up since then, they admit that the National Airspace System (NAS) is a huge beast composed of more than 23 million lines of code, 50 computer languages, and more than 250 computer systems. The air traffic control system alone has 34,000 systems and facilities operated by 36,500 employees. These systems are located across the country and must work together to transmit data 24 hours a day.

Jane Garvey, administrator of the FAA, testified before Congress that the "Y2K problem can affect NAS systems in a variety of ways. Software, hardware, or embedded code in NAS systems can be date sensitive."

To illustrate this, she discussed how one surveillance radar could affect the entire system:

Each of our twenty air traffic control centers has en route surveillance radar equipment, or ARSR, that monitors en route traffic in the system. The ARSR has a cooling pump system that turns on automatically to prevent the system from overheating. The computer code that initiates the cooling system is date dependent and, therefore, affected by Y2K. If the code is not Y2K compliant, the cooling system will not turn on at the correct day and time, and the ASRS could overheat and shut down. If this were to happen, air traffic controllers would have to monitor and separate aircraft the old-fashioned way, by altitude and time. This would slow down the system while air traffic is either rerouted or deliberately delayed to maintain safety.

Both the airlines and the FAA will ground aircraft rather than have them fly if a glitch of any kind is suspected, Y2K or otherwise. That is why I am not too worried about planes dropping out of the sky. Airlines and aircraft manufacturers have been checking all avionics in their planes for quite some time. (Boeing has been working on the Y2K problem for more than five years.) United Airlines, for example, discovered that the data management system in its older model 767 aircraft would not roll over on January 1, 2000, so they are replacing all these systems at a cost of $6 million.

What about other methods of travel? John Koskinen has said he has no faith in railroads being Y2K compliant by December 31 ("We are deeply concerned about the railroads. We have no indication that they are going to make it."—January 11, 1999), so I guess Amtrak is out of the question. I cannot speak on the safety of subway systems or city commuter trains, although I have heard whisperings about possible rail-switching problems. If this is true, then accidents are inevitable.

That leaves cars. Although many of today's vehicles have on-board microprocessors to operate and monitor various functions, I have yet to learn of any Y2K related glitches. (There was a press release circulated recently warning about problems in Cadillacs, but it turned out to be a hoax.) The more likely issue for drivers will be traffic lights. These red-yellow-green indicators rely on embedded systems to maintain the proper cycles required for weekdays and weekends. If they are not Y2K compliant, you could find yourself sitting at a light for what will seem like an hour before it finally changes. Worse yet, an intersection could have a four-way green light. So be careful! Look and look again before driving through an intersection.

TIP 54 *Be prepared to get around without a car*.

If the distribution system collapses and gas stations run out of fuel, you may end up with a $15,000 paperweight parked in your driveway. (The same holds true if there is a prolonged power blackout: gas pumps operate on electricity.)

So the question then becomes, how will you get to work? to the store? Well, get in shape and buy yourself a comfortable pair of shoes, because unless you are disabled, you will be doing quite a bit of walking.

Other viable forms of transportation include bicycling, roller-skating, and, one of my favorites, horseback riding.

TIP 55 *Improve your home's overall security*.

Do a security check of your home, paying attention to the following items. While doing the walk-around, put yourself in the shoes of a criminal. How would he try to gain access? What security weaknesses would *he* target?

Indoors

Do the main doors have dead-bolt locks? Does the basement door?

Are there any hinges that show on the *outside?*

Are the doors at least 1³/₄ inch thick and made of solid wood or reinforced with metal?

What shape is the doorjamb in? Does it need repair?

How tight is the seal when your doors are closed? Can you jiggle the door inward more than ¹/₈ inch?

Are there side windows on either side of a door that would allow someone to break in, reach through, and unlock the door?

Can someone gain access through a mail slot, dryer vent, or pet entrance?

Do you keep a spare key outside in a place where it will be easily found?

Do you have a peephole on your front door? If so, what can you see when looking out through it? Are there any blind spots?

Go room to room and look out the windows. Is there anything blocking your view? Just exactly what can you see and how far away? Does your view have any blind spots? If so, will using mirrors correct it?

Do you have any alarms on your doors or windows?

Are there alarm system stickers on your windows? If so, consider removing them if the power goes out. Otherwise, burglars will target your home since they know the alarms will not work without electricity.

Do all windows lock securely?

Outdoors

Are there nearby bushes or dense vegetation that someone could hide behind?

Is there a clear zone around your home or building that will allow you or your neighbors to see someone approaching?

How high up are the first floor windows? Do they allow easy access?

Do you have any basement windows? If so, how secure are they?

Does outdoor lighting completely illuminate your yard?
   How far out?
Are there any lightbulbs that need to be replaced?
Are there any dark zones that need to be illuminated with
   additional lighting?
If you have a bulkhead, how secure is it?

When you complete your inspection and have identified the
weaknesses, either correct them yourself or consult with a security company to have them install locks and nonelectric intruder alarms. Do not go crazy purchasing every gizmo under
the sun. The goal here is simply to improve the level of your
home's basic security so as to discourage hooligans from approaching.

TIP 56 *Protect your valuables*.

   Considering that you may increase your emergency
holdings of gold, silver, and cash in preparation for Y2K, you
need to take additional precautions. First of all, do not talk
about or show anyone your money, jewelry, gems, coins, or
bullion. You do not want to invite theft.
   Second, do not store all your valuables together. If someone
breaks in and finds your valuables, he has found them all. Instead, split the valuables up into smaller bundles and store
them separately.
   Third, store your valuables in safe, inconspicuous places
such as the freezer or a hollow book. You can also buy special
storage containers, such as fake household cleaning cans (e.g.,
furniture polish) and fake videotape boxes. If you opt to use a
safe, make sure that it is fire resistant and that it is small
enough so that you can hide it. If it is too large, then bolt it to
the floor to make it difficult for a burglar to walk off with it.
   As for bank safe-deposit boxes, they are not a bad idea, but
if there is an extended "bank holiday" you will not have easy
access to your belongings.

Fourth, do not hide your valuables in a moist location. Although gold will not tarnish, silver will. Cash—Federal Reserve notes—can deteriorate over time, even though the paper is specially treated for dampness. If you must store your valuables in a wet location, then seal the items in Ziplok baggies first.

Fifth, if you decide to bury some of your valuables do *not* let people see you do it! Recently, a couple in Florida buried their life savings in the backyard. It was gone within 24 hours. Someone probably observed them burying the strongbox.

After burying your valuables, scatter handfuls of BBs all over the hole and surrounding area. Cover a very wide area. This will deter any metal detector enthusiast from finding and digging up your belongings. As he approaches, he will suddenly hear hundreds of targets ringing in his earphones.

TIP 57 *Be ready to defend yourself.*

Since Y2K has the power to potentially wreak havoc on society, you need to be prepared to defend yourself. If the economy crashes, then those individuals who did not prepare for Y2K may—out of anger, thirst, or hunger—have to survive by stealing from those who did prepare. This could be especially true in cities, where the poor may prey on the middle class and the rich.

What can you do to protect yourself, your family, and your assets from violent criminals? 1) Do not talk about your assets; 2) be low-key in your dress and outward appearance; 3) travel in groups; 4) appear to be confident, alert, and assertive; 5) pay attention to your surroundings and stay away from potentially dangerous locations (e.g., parking garages, elevators, alleys, dirt roads); 6) trust your gut instinct—if you feel nervous or anxious, move! It is Mother Nature's proven million-year-old alarm system going off. Listen to it; 7) ensure that your home is secure.

On a more violent response scale, you can take self-defense

CHECK IT OUT . . . YOURSELF

Generator information
    209.52.183.182/agitator/Generator/pointers.htm
    www.gen-tran.com
    www.northern-online.com

Nonelectric heating appliances (e.g., woodstoves)
    hearth.com
    www.wood-heat.com/index.htm
    www.chimneys.com
    www.vermontcastings.com
    discountstove.com
    www.gamanet.org/consumer/ventfree
    www.toyostove.com
    www.lehmans.com
    www.gulland.ca

Universal Radio, Inc., 800-431-3939
Firearms and self-defense
    www.bev.net:10080/community/shawnee/gunbuyer.html
    www.defend-net.com/paxton

BTU calculator
    hearth.com/calc/btucalc.html

---

training or a course in martial arts such as karate or judo. A number of gyms, colleges, YMCAs, police departments, and health clubs offer such training programs.

You can also carry Mace, pepper spray, or a 20,000-volt stun gun. Be certain, though, that you receive instruction on how to properly use these items. The last thing you want to do if you are surrounded by a gang is spray yourself in the eyes with pepper spray.

And last, you can resort to using a firearm to defend yourself. More and more people are going this route.

I grew up with firearms, so I support the Second Amendment. I am also a staunch advocate of firearm safety. Rifles, handguns, and shotguns do *not* belong in the hands of untrained people! If you buy a firearm to protect yourself, get the proper training on how to handle, clean, and safely store it. If you have children at home, you are responsible for keeping firearms out of their hands! Always have the weapon under your direct control or locked.

Educate your older children (8 +) in gun safety just in case they somehow get their mitts on your or someone else's gun. Massad F. Ayoob, an expert in lethal force, has a book titled *Gunproof Your Children*. It is an excellent resource for teaching your children about guns. You can order the book by writing to: Lethal Force Institute, PO Box 122, Concord, NH 03302. Ayoob also teaches a variety of firearms and self-defense courses nationwide that you may be interested in.

If you are interested in buying a firearm for self-defense, then I suggest that you do two things. First, buy *Justifiable Homicide* written by retired deputy sheriff Denny Hansen, editor of *SWAT Magazine*. The book ($13.95) details the legal implications of shooting.

Second, purchase a handgun—a revolver to be more precise. Why a revolver and not an automatic? Most attacks—and gunfights—take place within a 25-foot range. In that distance, you need to be able to quickly pull your gun, aim, and fire. A revolver will allow you to do just that. Automatics, however, must be charged first to put a bullet in the chamber (unless you are carrying the weapon in this state). This requires the use of both hands, which you may or may not be able to do at the time. Even if you do charge the automatic, the bullet could stovepipe (i.e., stick up vertically) and jam the weapon. Guess what? You are on the ground by now with the attacker possibly beating you to death.

Thus, in most close encounters like this, you want to be able to just point and shoot. A revolver allows you to do that; it is idiot-proof.

Purchase nothing smaller than a .38 caliber. (This is ideal for many women, by the way. If you will carry the pistol in a purse, consider a .38 that has an *internal* hammer. This will prevent the gun from getting snagged on items in the purse.) The .38 Special is easy to handle and has a variety of ammunition you can buy for target shooting and self-defense. For greater power, consider buying a .357 or .44 Magnum with a minimum four-inch barrel. If you get a shorter barrel, it is extremely loud and less accurate to shoot.

If you insist on purchasing an automatic, then stick with either 9-mm or .45 ACP. These calibers have proven themselves over the years and you can find ammo just about everywhere.

For home defense purposes, the shotgun is King. The sound of someone racking a round in a shotgun gets everyone's immediate and full attention. I suggest either a 20- or 12-gauge shotgun. If an intruder enters your home, use rounds that are specially designed for indoor use. That way the pellets will not penetrate the walls of three rooms, endangering other family members. (Note: Similar rounds have been developed for handguns. They are often referred to as shot shells.)

For hunting purposes, a .308, 30–30, or 30.06 rifle with a mounted scope will serve the purpose. Shotguns can also be used—sabot slugs for animals and shot for birds.

How many rounds should you buy? That is entirely up to you and your anxiety over how bad the world is going to become. I know of people who have stockpiled as few as four 50-round boxes and those who have nearly 10,000 rounds in military ammo containers. Regardless of the quantity, you should practice on a routine basis to keep your shooting skills honed.

Before buying any weapon, check with the laws in your state regarding ownership, concealed carry, and lethal force. And remember, gun laws can change from county to county, so be careful where you travel, otherwise you may find yourself being arrested for illegal possession.

TIP 58 *Prevent fires and explosions from happening.*

As you begin stockpiling items for Y2K, you will undoubtedly have more fire hazards than normal in your home—boxes of matches, extra gasoline containers, 20-pound propane tanks, et cetera. The risk of fire will also increase during a power blackout since you will be using alternate heating and lighting sources, such as propane heaters and candles or lamps. To minimize the possibility of an explosion or fire, follow these tips:

- Keep fuels stored in approved containers, and check for leaks on a regular basis.
- Fuel containers should be stored outside the home in a shed or garage. Do not leave containers outdoors in direct sunlight.
- Keep burning candles and oil/kerosene lamps out of the reach of children and pets and away from curtains and shades.
- Have several fire extinguishers in your home, and store them where they can be quickly reached. Check them twice a year to make sure that they are fully charged, as indicated by the gauge.
- Install battery-powered smoke detectors and carbon monoxide detectors in your home.
- Have chemical extinguisher sticks like Chimfex on hand to snuff out a chimney fire if one begins. To reduce the risk of a chimney fire, have your flue cleaned of creosote each year.
- If you buy new propane tanks, make sure they are properly purged before filling them the first time.

On the Financial Front

IT'S TIME TO GET YOUR HOUSEHOLD IN ORDER

I'm truly scared about the year 2000 (problem).
—Robert Stanky, Manager
Fidelity Magellan Fund

I've been a hard sell on the Y2K problem,
but I am now convinced this problem is real, although
its dimensions are impossible to define. The only
thing that is sure is that it is big, very big!
—Howard Ruff, financial guru
Publisher, *Ruff Times*

Y2K could turn the financial world upside down. Even people who do not believe in Y2K itself understand this. Why? Because they know people, by nature, do not like to lose their hard-earned money and, thus, may pull money out of banks and investments out of the stock market to preserve what they have, in fear of losing it to the millennium bug. Although the withdrawals will be done for reasons of safety, the action could severely stress the financial system.

In the past year, I have spoken with many non-Y2K believers and, to a person, they clearly see the danger in this. As a result, many of them are now taking steps to protect their own financial assets from the so-called Y2Kaos.

So guess what? Now everyone is paranoid: both the Y2K believers *and* the Y2K nonbelievers. The financial system is beginning to groan.

There are a number of financial matters you need to address. Keep in mind as you read this chapter that I am not a certified financial planner. I just happen to have a strong interest in finance. Thus, the advice presented here represents my own opinion—albeit influenced by personal experience and input from professionals. Before taking any action with your own assets, you are strongly encouraged to sit down with an advisor to discuss your intentions.

TIP 59 *Protect your property*.

Where Y2K is concerned, you need to focus primarily on two areas: theft and fire. Here are a few things you can do:

- Have your jewelry and expensive belongings insured against theft.
- Improve your home security efforts to thwart burglary. (See Tip 55.)
- Mark valuable and easily stolen property , such as televisions and camera equipment, with a personal identification number.
- Store cash, precious metals, and gems away in a hidden safe. (See Tip 56.)
- Install battery-operated smoke alarms to alert you to a fire.
- Buy extra fire extinguishers to handle fires started by a woodstove, burning candle, or oil lamp.

TIP 60 *Photograph and inventory household valuables*.

If you heeded my advice in Chapter 3, when you did an assessment of your home, you should already have a list of your valuables. If you did not, here's another plea for you to do so. The inventory will not only give you an idea of what you have but it will be helpful in substantiating an insurance claim in the event you are robbed or your home is destroyed. It will also help you determine what items you could use for bartering purposes should you ever find yourself running short of money.

When conducting an inventory, go from room to room and record on paper each item of value, when you purchased it, the price you paid for it (if you can recall), and what it is likely to be worth today. Take a photograph of the room to show the items in their normal position. For more valuable pieces, such as a rare antique, it is a good idea to take a close-up photo as well to substantiate its condition. The photographs establish that you indeed do own the valuables.

If you have access to a video camera, then videotape each room while narrating what is being filmed. This is much faster than doing it by pen and paper or camera. If you do not own a video camera, borrow one from a friend or rent one for a weekend.

If you have receipts for any item (including canceled checks), gather them together in one location or file folder and have photocopies made. Do the same for any appraisal you have had done for jewelry, antiques, collections, or artwork.

When the inventory is completed, make two copies of the written list and photographs (or videotape) and store one set in a place outside your home, such as at a parent's home. Make sure family members know where to find this inventory in case something happens to you.

TIP ⑥⑴ *Buy insurance ... if you still can.*

It is imperative that you review your insurance needs, whether you own your home or rent an apartment. Although most policies cover damage from riots, glass breakage, fire, theft, and plumbing problems, there are a variety of Y2K-related issues that you should consider getting additional insurance coverage for:

Food spoilage—Covers the contents of your freezer or refrigerator in case of a power failure. Coverage limit: $1,000.

Lock Replacement—Covers the replacement costs if some-one steals your house keys. Limit: $250.

Fire Department Service Charge—If you live in a remote area, this covers the fee for fire departments to protect your home from fire. Limit: $500.

Debris Removal—Covers the cost to remove debris from your property following a disaster. Limit: Varies.

High-Value Insurance—Covers the theft of expensive items like jewelry, firearms, and fine arts. Limit: $2,500+ per identi-fied item (e.g., stamps, securities, firearm, jewelry, boats, gold).

Water-Bed Liability—Covers damage done to your home from a leaking water bed. Limit: Varies.

Unfortunately, many insurance companies are no longer of-fering policies that have a Y2K tie-in, such as a personal com-puter policy. (Lloyd's of London has estimated that global claims could top $1 trillion dollars.) If you have an existing insurance policy, you may receive a letter from your insurer clarifying that Y2K problems are *not* covered. This happened to Nationwide Insurance policy holders in September 1998. The letter, in part, read:

It is important for you to know it was never intended that computer failures relating to programming limitations would be covered by commercial or personal lines insurance policies. Nationwide is consistent with the insurance industry in this re-spect.

Losses due to year 2000 problems may not be covered be-cause, among other reasons, they are not fortuitous losses. Fortuitous losses are those not anticipated or expected. Loss, damage, or injury resulting from failure to address the year 2000 problem is not a fortuitous event.

In other words, if there is a Y2K-induced power outage in January 2000 and your water pipes freeze and burst, you may not be covered under your current insurance policy. What do you do? Call your insurance agent today and get clarification on what will and what will not be covered by your policy.

Then, if possible, take corrective action to minimize damage to your home from noncovered Y2K events.

TIP 62 *Make copies of important documents*.

Can you prove you are the rightful owner of your home or car? Can you prove that you have paid your taxes? Under normal circumstances, you could visit the agency that has your records on computer and quickly resolve either issue. But what if those documents become mixed up or lost due to a Y2K computer glitch? Then what will you do???

For this reason, you need to make copies of all important documents and safely store them in a place where you have access to them. Review the following list and see which documents apply to you:

Financial

IRS tax returns (three to seven years) (Note: If you need to get a copy of an old return, file IRS Form 4506 "Request for Copy of Tax Form." The charge for each return is $14.)

state and local income tax returns (three to seven years)

investment account statements (e.g., IRA, 401(k), mutual funds)

stocks, bonds, and other investment vehicles (actual certificates)

bank account statements

credit card statement (1 year)

credit card terms and conditions

safe deposit box (terms and conditions, plus rental receipt)

retirement accounts

titles to equipment

unemployment benefits record

Home

mortgage (application and most recent statements that show principal, escrow, et cetera)

home equity loan (application and most recent statements that
   show outstanding balance, interest, et cetera)
deed
property survey (aka plat)
rental agreement (plus canceled checks)
home improvement receipts
title search
property tax records (three years)
homeowner's insurance policy
renter's insurance policy
major appliance warranties
household bills (e.g., heating, telephone, cable TV, electricity)

Personal
birth and death certificates of family members
power of attorney (medical and legal)
passport and visas
adoption papers
marriage certificate
divorce papers and related legal documentation (e.g., child
   support)
immunization records
church records (e.g., baptism)
organizational membership
pedigrees for pets and livestock
driver's license
auto registration and insurance
loan agreements
lease agreements
wills and trusts
inheritance documents
life insurance policy
health insurance policy
auto registration
paycheck stubs (one to two years)
business records (if self-employed)
military service records

medical records
dental records
credit report
school and college transcripts
certification documents
social security earnings and benefits statement

When you have gathered the necessary documents, store them in a file cabinet, safe deposit box, or fireproof safe. Then update them at least once a year, discarding any outdated documents and adding files for new policies, major purchases, investments, et cetera.

TIP 63 *Get a copy of your credit report*.

Your personal credit rating is arguably the most important asset you own. It not only determines whether or not you qualify for a loan of any sort, but it can in some cases influence a company's decision to hire you for a particular job. Since the credit system is extremely dependent on computer technology, you must get a copy of your credit history both *before* and *after* January 1, 2000. If a computer makes a mistake or if your credit file is deleted because of a Y2K problem, you will be able to preserve your credit rating.

There are three major credit reporting bureaus you need to contact:

- Equifax, Atlanta, GA, 800-685-1111
- Experian, Allen, TX, 888-397-3742
- Trans Union, Springfield, PA, 800-888-4213

Do not assume that if one agency's credit report on you is correct that the other's will be too. You need to check all three since they gather their information from different sources.

TIP 64 *Correct errors immediately*.

Review your bank statements, financial records, and credit reports with a fine-tooth comb. If you find a mistake or omission, bring it to the company's attention immediately by telephone and then follow up with a written letter to cover yourself. Pay particular attention to any 00 errors that may show up in a birth date or expiration date.

This happened to one person I know: She was talking to her bank about transferring an IRA to their institution, when the representative, who was reviewing her account information, politely asked if she had been born on January 1, 1900. The computer incorrectly had her birth date as—you guessed it—01/01/00. "Well, you didn't sound like you were ninety-nine years old," the representative said laughing, when told the information was wrong.

This incident was minor, but an incorrect birth date on your records can cause more serious problems. For instance, it could adversely affect your ability to receive a welfare benefit or to get a lower auto insurance premium. Both of these examples are age dependent.

TIP 65 *Get a copy of your Social Security earnings and benefit statement.*

Many people overlook this document when gathering their financial records. Yet it is an important document because it tells you how long you have worked, how much you have earned and, more importantly, how much you will receive each month from Social Security when you retire. If the millennium bug munches this record up—in spite of Social Security's assurances that it will not happen—you will have trouble trying to prove 20 to 40 years worth of work history. That is why you need a copy of it in your files.

To order your earnings and benefit statement, call 800-772-1213. Ask for a copy of SSA form #7004. When you receive the form, fill it out and mail back. You will receive your statement in four to six weeks.

Do this *before* and *after* January 1, 2000, and compare the results to make certain that no errors have occurred. It is a good idea to continue this effort at least once a year thereafter.

If you presently receive Social Security checks, keep a copy of all your checks in a file folder. If the payment is made by electronic deposit, keep a copy of your bank statements and the deposit slip you receive in the mail. This establishes an ongoing sequence of documents that will validate your account and help settle any dispute that may arise as a result of Y2K.

TIP 66 *Get a copy of your military service record.*

If you are a veteran of the armed forces, request a copy of your military service and medical records in case Y2K tampers with the Department of Veterans Affairs' computer files. By having a hard copy on file at home, you will be able to prove your military service history and continue to receive the benefits you currently receive.

To order your file, send a written request to:

National Personnel Records Center
9700 Page Boulevard
St. Louis, MO 63132-5200

In your letter, provide the following information: full name, mailing address, date and place of birth, social security number, service number, branch of service, and the dates during which you served.

TIP 67 *Determine how ready your employer is for Y2K.*

Will you have a job in 2000? That's the million-dollar question, because a number of businesses will have to lay off personnel if Y2K causes even minor disruptions to the manufacturing and distribution sectors. In fact, Software Productivity Research, in its landmark study "The Economic Impact of the Year 2000 Computer Software Problem" anticipates a great number of businesses actually failing:

- Five of the Fortune 500 companies
- 1,500 to 2,100 midsized companies (These firms employ 1,000 to 10,000 people each)
- 180,000 small companies (These firms employ less than 100 people each)

If the report's prediction comes true, then *millions* of Americans will be standing in the unemployment line. This is why you need to find out just how prepared your company is for Y2K. If it is poorly prepared, then you might want to consider changing jobs and finding employment with a stronger, better-prepared company. Another option is to impress your supervisors so much by taking on new projects et cetera that they would feel reluctant to fire you later on.

How do you find out what progress your company has made in its Y2K preparation efforts? First, find out whether or not there is a Y2K committee and, if so, who it is staffed by. (If there is no Y2K office or coordinator, that in itself is a big red flag!) Get to know those individuals or people who know them, and find out what they are like and whether they feel good progress is being made.

Second, read company newsletters, E-mails and memos that address Y2K to find out what is and what is not being done. If you work for a company that is publicly traded on the stock market, read its 10Q and 10E statements. Both documents are required by the Securities and Exchange Commission to disclose the financial impact of Y2K remediation.

Third, look for signs that things are going poorly. For example, if you learn that the company is still assessing the problem and had not begun any remediation or testing, it's a bad sign. The same holds true if there is talk about replacing Y2K bugged systems instead of fixing the computer code. Ditto, if there is no contingency planning being done.

TIP 68 *Identify risks to your income.*

"**W**hy is there so much month left at the end of the money?"

Although we all laugh at this, we also know that it is quite true. Most of us, in fact, live from paycheck to paycheck. This practice could become even more severe and stressful if Y2K messes up computer functions. There are a number of ways it can threaten your income, including:

Unemployment—If your company files bankruptcy as a result of a computer glitch, you will be fortunate to walk out the door with one last paycheck in hand.

Late Payment—Your company may not be able to cut checks if payroll computers are not working properly. This has already happened: In January 1999 11 states were delayed in distributing unemployment benefit checks as a result of Y2K problems.

If you are retired, you should anticipate delays in receiving your social security checks. Although social security announced in December 1998 that is was Y2K compliant, it does not actually mail or electronically deposit your checks! That is done by the Financial Management Service (FMS), an agency within the Treasury Department. And FMS is *not* Y2K compliant! In fact, Treasury Secretary Robert Rubin is worried about the agency: "The only bureau left with truly serious (Y2K) issues is (FMS). That bureau, which handles a wide range of financial transactions for almost every government agency—including the administration of the Electronic Federal Tax Payment System—continues to be 'the area we're most concerned about.' "

Direct Deposit—If you have your company electronically deposit your paycheck into your bank account, you may or may not receive it. The computer transfer system could send it to the wrong account, or not at all. (See Tip 71.)

Calculations—Banks and finance computers perform a variety of date-sensitive functions, including calculating interest and other charges, and monitoring deposit, loan, and lease payments. If a computer glitch occurs, you may not receive the full amount owed you in a paycheck, Social Security check, pension payment, et cetera.

Clearance—Computers are used to clear deposited checks. If there is a delay, it could be days or even weeks before you have "money" in the bank to withdraw or write checks against.

Mail Disruption—If Y2K disrupts the U.S. Postal Service's ability to electronically sort though millions of letters each day, it could take several weeks for you to receive a Social Security check, company dividend check, or unemployment check by mail.

As you can see, it would not take much for Y2K to easily disrupt your household's cash flow. For this reason, you need to reduce your debt and increase your savings. Strive to have enough money to take care of expenses—food, rent or mortgage, power, heat—for at least two to three months.

TIP 69 *Pay down your debt.*

As long as you carry a debt on your credit card—$50 or $5,000, it doesn't matter—the money you have in a bank or wallet is not your own. Adding insult to injury, you are giving people an additional 13 to 21 percent of your hard-earned money.

So stop it. Today.

The millennium bug could cause a severe worldwide recession, at least that's what Ed Yardeni of Deutsche Bank in New York is predicting. If you lose your job as a result of a deflationary economy, how are you going to pay off your debt? Your creditors will still want the monthly payment regardless of Y2K or whether or not you are employed. (Note: At this writing, Congress is considering legislation to protect citizens from Y2K gliches that result in late payment to creditors.) Are you willing to declare bankruptcy? Are you willing to lose everything you have . . . when you need it the most?

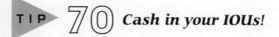

TIP 70 *Cash in your IOUs!*

Although it is charitable of you to extend a loan to a family member or friend when he needs it, the time has come for you to stop being so generous. No one knows for certain just how serious Y2K's impact on the economy will be, but if a recession or depression rolls in, then you can kiss your loan good-bye.

So collect what you can now, and be willing to shrug your shoulders to the rest of it. If you want to get mad, then direct your anger at Y2K—but cherish your relationships.

TIP 71 *Be leery of electronic fund transfers to make payments.*

In the last decade, automatic electronic payment has become increasingly popular. Instead of writing out checks to pay the bills, you simply authorized your bank to electronically send payment directly to the mortgage company, credit card firm, or retail store. This process saved you time, headaches, and postage.

But now that Y2K has reared its ugly head, this technology could metamorphose into a monster. For instance, if there are any delays in the system as a result of Y2K, your creditors may not receive payment on time and, thus, your credit rating could be tarnished. The computer system could also accidentally wire your payment to someone in Iceland or Tuvalu. (He may be happy, but you won't.) In the worst-case scenario, the system could even empty your bank account, leaving you with not even a penny!

TIP 72 *Prepay bills two months in advance.*

There is a reason behind this tip: the postal service relies heavily on technology to sort and deliver *millions* of pieces of mail every day. If Y2K messes things up, then the mail may have to be sorted the old-fashioned way, by hand. What normally takes three work days to accomplish could then take two weeks or longer.

The situation could be made much worse if a distribution slowdown occurs, since there would be fewer vehicles and airplanes to move mail across the country. Then, to send a letter coast-to-coast could take as long as six weeks.

This means that even if you mail a payment a month in advance of its due date, it could still arrive late—and, once again, your credit rating could be temporarily tarnished.

Why should you care? After all, you *did* pay in time and the delay is *not* your fault, right? Creditors simply don't care. If they do not receive payment, they come after you—Y2K or no Y2K. Remember, their existence will be on the line then, too.

So rather than have to deal with harassing phone calls from bill collectors, mail your payments two months in advance. This process works best on those bills that invoice you the same amount each month, such as cable television, storage unit fee, insurance premium, and heating fuel (flat-rate plan).

TIP 73 *Keep credit card receipts.*

Keep all your credit card receipts and compare them against the statements when they come in by mail. Make sure that all the purchases are correct, and that you have not been double billed or had someone enter the wrong dollar amount.

If you spot an error, immediately notify the credit card issuer by telephone. The customer service representative will instruct you on what you need to do to have a correction made. Usually, you are required to submit a written complaint, along with copies of any documentation (i.e., receipts!) that will substantiate your claim. In the meanwhile, the credit card company will immediately credit your account for the disputed amount until it has a chance to review your case. This means you do not pay any interest charges on the disputed amount.

TIP **74** *Protect yourself from financial fraud.*

Identity fraud is a growing problem in the United States. In 1997, the U.S. Secret Service reported $745 million in actual losses attributed to identity fraud.

In one case, Bob Hartle, an Arizona resident, had someone run up credit card charges and loans in excess of $100,000! This same individual, while posing as Hartle, filed a $45,000 bankruptcy, received a speeding ticket after being involved in an accident, obtained employment (and was subsequently fired!), opened numerous bank accounts, and failed to pay any federal or state taxes.

How do you prevent someone from using *your* identity, assets, and credit to get what they want while destroying your life?

- Install a locked mailbox at home to deter mail theft.
- Have new bank checks mailed to a PO box so criminals cannot get their hands on them.
- Don't leave paid bills out in your mailbox to be picked up by the postal carrier; take them to a mailbox instead.
- Cancel and then destroy unused credit cards.
- Don't carry extra credit cards, birth certificate, passport, or Social Security card in your wallet or purse (except when absolutely necessary).
- When creating a password or PIN, never use your birth

date, Social Security number, middle name, pet's name, or consecutive numbers (e.g., 3456).

- Use your body to shield the ATM screen and keypad to prevent someone who is spying with binoculars from stealing your PIN.
- Never print your Social Security number on your bank checks.
- Tear up preapproved credit card offers that come through the mail before throwing them away. This prevents someone from going through your trash and applying for a credit card in your name.
- Use a permanent marker when filling out a check. That way a criminal cannot erase the "payable to" and dollar amount, and replace it with his name and a five-digit number.

If your ATM card is stolen or compromised, get a new card, account number, and password. If your checks are ever stolen, contact your bank to place a stop-payment on all outstanding checks and report the theft to police. To find out if there is any activity on your account as a result of fraud, call one of the following check verification companies:

CheckRite	800-766-2748
Chexsystems	800-428-9623
Equifax	800-437-5120
SCAN	800-262-7771
Telecheck	800-710-9898
National Processing Co.	800-526-5380

TIP 75 *Ask your financial service provider how it will deal with Y2K.*

Visit your bank and speak with a customer service representative, a loan officer, or the comptroller. Ask what the bank is doing to minimize its risk exposure to Y2K, and what contingency plans it has drawn up. Ask if the bank has increased its *cash reserves* to handle a sudden increase in withdrawals. If they have, find out how much of an increase it really is. Most banks have only between 1 percent and 3 percent of their holdings available in cash. The higher this percentage, the stronger the bank. Do not hesitate to request this information. It is public information, and banks are required to provide it to you when asked.

If the bank has not boosted its cash reserves, find out if they have drafted any emergency rules that, when put into effect, would limit withdrawal amounts (e.g., $50 per person per day).

Also, ask the bank what type of backup records are kept in case of an emergency. How would these records be used to identify and correct problems that affect your checking or savings account?

If you are not comfortable with any responses given by the bank representative—or if he belittle your concerns—close your account and take your business elsewhere.

Banks and credit unions aside, you should call other financial institutions you are involved with—mutual funds, brokerages, investment firms—and find out what they are doing to prepare for Y2K. It is your money that is in their hands, and you have a right to know what they are doing to protect it. All publicly traded companies are now required to disclose this information on their Securities and Exchange Commission (SEC) reports. You can learn more about this by visiting the SEC database at www.sec.gov/news/y2k/y2kreps.htm

TIP 76 *Have cash on hand.*

Consider the fact that there are not enough dollar bills in circulation right now to allow everyone to turn their bank accounts into stacks of $20, $50, or $100 bills. In fact, if only 5 percent of the population tried to do just that, the banking system would allegedly be ruined.

Anticipating that people may become apprehensive about Y2K and withdraw a portion, if not all, of their money from banks, the Federal Reserve has asked the U.S. Treasury to print an additional $50 billion in currency, raising the level to $200 billion. (Note: Contrary to popular belief, the Federal Reserve is *not* a government agency. It is a privately held corporation that was established in 1913 by President Wilson to control the flow of currency. Alan Greenspan, the current chairman, answers to no one, not even Congress. He decides if interest rates go up—thereby constricting currency—or down—expanding currency.)

Individual banks are also worried about Y2K: they are expecting crowds to line up and withdraw their money by the end of 1999, thereby causing a bank run. To avoid this, many banks are creating contingency plans that outline what withdrawal limits will be levied, and under what conditions they will close their doors for a bank "holiday."

Because cash may be needed to pay for food and other necessities in a Y2K environment, you are encouraged to create an at-home cash stash. Even the federal government admits this may be necessary. Although they recommend $500 per family, others advocate that you have enough cash on hand to take care of expenses for two to three months, or even longer.

Begin doing this today, and spread it out over several months rather than all at once. Have your cash in small bills—ones, fives, tens, and twenties—in case stores have a difficult time making change. And speaking of change, have 5 to 10 percent of your money in coins.

If you do not have a large savings account, then begin setting aside $50 to $100 from each paycheck. Other ways to raise cash include selling belongings you do not need or marketing your skilled services to businesses on a part-time basis in addition to your normal job.

TIP ▶ 77 *Acquire gold and silver.*

Historically, when times become difficult, people lose confidence in currency and seek the safety that gold and silver offer. Since Y2K could trigger a recession or even another Great Depression, you should consider acquiring gold and silver as a hedge against calamity. Before you do, however: 1) pay down your debt and credit cards; and 2) acquire food, water, and other basic necessities to survive Y2K.

You can buy gold in three different forms: ingots, numismatics, and bullion coins. How do they differ? An ingot is a small bar of gold that weighs 1, 5, 10, 32, 100, or 400 troy ounces. The bars can be difficult to sell since a buyer needs proof that an ingot is not gold-plated lead. Hence, an assay is often required.

Numismatics are collector-quality coins that are graded and priced according to their condition, rarity, and gold content and purity. Because of this, you nearly always pay more for the coin than just its gold value. Premiums can run 200 percent or higher.

Bullion coins are coins minted by governments solely for their gold content and purity.

Of the three, focus your initial efforts on acquiring the gold bullion coins. They are easier to purchase than gold ingots, they are less expensive to buy than numismatic coins, and their purity is guaranteed by the government. Additionally, they fluctuate in price with the market price of gold. So if gold goes up, the value of a Maple Leaf or Panda coin is likely to go up as well, although perhaps not by the same proportion.

There are a number of gold bullion coins on the market, including:

Chinese Pandas	.999 pure gold	
Canadian Maple Leafs	.999	"
Australian Kangaroos	.999	"
Austrian Philharmonics	.999	"
Isle of Man Persian Cats	.999	"
British Britannias	.917	"
American Eagles	.917	"
South African Kruggerands	.917	"
Mexican Pesos	.900	"

The American Eagle, as with a few other gold bullion coins, is available in different sizes: 1 ounce, $\frac{1}{2}$ ounce, $\frac{1}{4}$ ounce and $\frac{1}{10}$ ounce. This allows you to buy coins that will fit your budget. At this writing, the spot gold price is $290 and the coins are selling for:

1 ounce	$311.50
$\frac{1}{2}$ ounce	$159.75
$\frac{1}{4}$ ounce	$ 81.75
$\frac{1}{10}$ ounce	$ 35.00

If you are a math whiz, you have already figured out that to buy an ounce of any of these coins costs more than the actual gold price. That is because retail sellers, commercial brokers, and the U.S. Mint add a premium for their time and effort to either produce or acquire the bullion coins for you. The premium is higher for the smaller coins—20 percent for $\frac{1}{10}$ ounce coins and 15 percent for $\frac{1}{4}$ ounce coins—simply because the U.S. Mint has to make more of them for each ounce, instead of striking just one 1-ounce coin (i.e., ten $\frac{1}{10}$-ounce coins). The process is slower and more labor intensive.

You can buy gold bullion coins in two ways. The first is to visit a local bank or coin shop. The problem is, they may not have any coins in stock, so you will have to wait until they do. The second way is faster and easier: you call one of several national brokers and place an order.

So what gold bullion coins should you begin acquiring? Well, according to Linda Gorman at Resource Consultants Inc. (Tempe, AZ, 800-494-4149), the most popular gold coins as of February 1999 were: American Eagles, Austrian Philharmonics, and South African Krugerrands. So use that as a general guide.

If you are concerned that the American Eagles could be called in by the federal government, don't worry. Although gold has been confiscated three times in the past 200 years, it is not about to happen again. The most recent event occurred during the Great Depression: President Roosevelt signed an executive order in 1933 prohibiting the hoarding of all U.S.

gold coins. Americans were instructed to turn in their gold coins at an exchange rate of $35 an ounce. Foreign gold coins were exempt, as were investment-grade and rare coins. And if you had less than $100 worth of gold, face value, you did not have to turn it in either.

This confiscation is not likely to happen again, since the United States no longer operates by the gold standard it had back in 1933. In those days, you had the right to receive the face value of any banknote in gold. Hence, for example, a $10 bill could be exchanged at a bank for $10 worth of gold. When this gold standard was eliminated, there was no longer any reason for the government to control people's access to gold. This is why the danger of confiscation does not exist today. (As additional proof, the government allows people to have their IRAs in gold. And, furthermore, the U.S. Mint is the number-one seller of gold coins; it has no desire to cut off its profits.)

As for which size gold coins to buy, many advise the smaller coins—$1/4$ and $1/10$ ounce—for Y2K purposes, at least initially. This is because if a deflationary economy does occur, prices will fall. It will be easier to exchange a $1/10$ ounce gold coin for food than with a one-ounce coin. Additionally, as long as gold prices remain low, the premium for a small coin is less than it will be later on if the price of gold skyrockets.

As for silver, it too is available in various forms: ingots, bullion coins, and junk silver. The latter refers to coins that were minted and circulated in 1964 or earlier. These coins contain 90 percent silver. At the current spot silver price of about $5 per ounce, an old silver dime is worth about $.40; a quarter, $1; a half dollar, $2; and a dollar, $4.

Junk silver is generally sold by brokers and coin dealers in pouches with a total face value of $1,000 in dimes, quarters, et cetera. At the current silver price, a pouch sells for $5,350, which includes a small premium. This provides you with 715 ounces of actual silver.

Investors recommend that 30 to 50 percent of your precious-metal holdings should be in junk silver.

With regard to bullion silver coins (aka rounds), the .999 pure silver American Eagles are your best bet. The U.S. Mint sold 2.86 million ounces of them in 1998.

As with gold coins, there is a danger associated with silver coins: if the economy collapses and deflation sets in, the price of silver will fall. Gold, although it will also drop, tends to hold it's value.

Another drawback is that silver takes up more storage room than gold. At this time, an ounce of gold is 58 times more valuable than an ounce of silver. Thus, you can carry $1,000 worth of gold in just four coins (three 1-ounce coins and one half-ounce coin), but you would have to lug 200 1-ounce silver coins to equal the same amount.

How much silver and gold should you have in your possession? It depends on how anxious you are about Y2K and how much money you have to purchase the coins. In general, investment advisors recommend having at least 5 percent of your portfolio in precious metals that you actually can touch.

As for storage, keep the bullion coins in the plastic containers they come in—it protects them from damage and moisture. Wrap electrical tape around the outside of the containers holding the silver coins: you want to prevent air from seeping in and tarnishing the coins. (Gold does not tarnish.) And last, store the coins in a fireproof safe at home or in a bank safe deposit box. For safety's sake, divide the coins into several smaller stashes and then hide them in various places around your home. Some people even go so far as to bury them in waterproof containers on their property.

If you remember nothing else about precious metals, remember this: Your stash of gold and silver is *not* an investment! You need to consider the bullion as *insurance* against bad times, when either inflation roars in or the economy collapses. If you decide to add luster to your portfolio, do it soon: people are buying bullion coins like crazy. In 1998, the U.S. Mint sold an all-time record of 1.8 million ounces of gold. In previous years, sales were between 300,000 and 350,000 ounces per year.

TIP 78 *Avoid gemstones as a monetary asset.*

Although beautiful, easily portable, and valuable, gemstones are not where you want to store you money for emergency use. This is for three reasons:

1. Gems are difficult to identify. It takes a trained gemologist to correctly identify a ruby from a red garnet.
2. Gems are difficult to grade and price. The average person on the street simply cannot tell a high-quality stone from a low-quality stone (and he is not about to take your word on it!).
3. Since demand for gems decreases in economically bad times—people want food and water before they want a new ring—prices plummet, especially for semiprecious stones such as amethyst, opal, and garnet. Only the value of diamonds tends to hold.

The only exception to stockpiling gemstones as a means of money is if you are knowledgeable about gems and intend to do most of your trading with people who are equally educated.

TIP 79 *Take care of your stock market investments.*

Since 1997, when the majority of Americans learned about Y2K, there has been considerable apprehension about the possibility of the world's financial markets crashing. Instead of having this fear alleviated over time, it has actually become worse. Why?

Nondisclosure—Even though transfer agents, broker-dealers, investment advisers, and mutual funds are now required by federal law to disclose how ready their computer systems are for 2000, many elect not to do so. In fact, the Securities and Exchange Commission (SEC) says that more than half the companies in a sampling failed to disclose how much it is costing them to get their computer systems ready for Y2K, while close to half did not describe their contingency plans. Subsequently, the SEC has fined a number of firms.

This reluctance to release information is making investors nervous. (It also infuriates Senator Robert Bennett, who chastised Fortune 500 companies in February 1999 for being deliberately vague about their Y2K remediation efforts.) Many investors, in fact, are now selling a company's stocks or bonds if it refuses to discuss its Y2K contingency plans. They figure, why invest when, by the company's silence, they are admitting they have a problem with Y2K?

Y2K Cost—It is extremely expensive for a company to assess its computer systems for Y2K and then correct the bugs that are found. In fact, most companies severely underfinanced the costs when they began their efforts in 1997 and 1998. Because of this, firms—in a scramble to become Y2K compliant by December 31—have dramatically increased their spending and are now telling investors not to expect strong returns for the year.

CHECK IT OUT . . . YOURSELF

Personal finance
   www.ftc.gov/bcp/conline/pubs/alerts/y2k-finalrt.htm
   www.money.com
   www.bloomberg.com

Central Fund of Canada
   www.centralfund.com

Company Y2K compliance
   www.y2kalert.org
   www.tech2k.org
   www.willitwork.com
   home-3.worldonline.nl/~vegterda/
   www.y2kcertified.com

In a few severe instances, the cost to fix Y2K has been so expensive that companies with limited resources have actually been forced into bankruptcy. In these cases, investors lost everything.

Because of the prospect of lower returns, or even the outright loss of their money, investors are beginning to sell the stocks and bonds of rickety companies. Instead, they are investing in companies that have adequate resources to deal with Y2K problems.

Correction—A number of people have stated that the stock market is long overdue for a correction. Stocks are overpriced, with price-to-earnings ratios (P/E) of some company stocks being at all-time record highs of 30:1, 40:1, 50:1, and even 60:1! For comparison, the P/E ratio has traditionally been between 10 and 20. Some economists are now anticipating a 30 to 40 percent drop in the Dow in 1999. This decrease would be more severe than Black Monday, when on October 19, 1987, the market lost 23 percent of its value. Investors, hearing this prediction of an imminent market correction and witnessing the dramatic up-and-down surges of the market, are more anxious today than ever before. Thoughts of withdrawal are dancing through their heads.

For all of these reasons, you need to seriously review your investments and determine a strategy that will preserve your capital. Surely you do not want to see your profits get sucked down the Y2K cesspool?

There are several investment options available to you. If you are nervous about companies failing to rectify their Y2K problems, then consider taking these steps:

- Get out of risky investments (e.g., high tech, sector funds, emerging markets) and place your money in more conservative investment vehicles (e.g., treasury bonds, money market funds).
- If you are extremely worried and feel that a stock market meltdown is inevitable, then get out of the market entirely. Place your money in a bank CD or money market

account. (Your bank accounts are insured up to $100,000 by the FDIC in each bank.) IRAs can be transferred from a mutual fund to your bank.

- And, if you truly believe that society itself is going to collapse—teotwawki—then liquidate all your holdings, including retirement plans and bank savings accounts. If society does indeed fail, then so will FDIC and the U.S. government. Put a portion of your money into precious metals to hedge against this calamity. (Note: There is a penalty for withdrawing your retirement funds: a 20 percent withholding tax plus a 10 percent forfeiture. Also, be aware of the fact that if too many people liquidate their IRAs and other retirement plans at once, the government will probably step in and halt withdrawals.)

However, if you are more optimistic about Y2K and feel there might be good investment opportunities for you, consider these options:

- Reallocate your investment portfolio now so that you are invested in sectors that will perform well in a sour market. For a list of funds that perform well in a bear market—such as Rydex Ursa Fund and Robertson Stephens Contrarian Fund—visit: www.bearmarketcentral.com/mutualfunds.htm
- Another option is to park a portion of your money today in a money market fund—thereby protecting it somewhat from a volatile market—and then closely monitor the market for good buying opportunities as share prices fall.

TIP ⑧⓪ *Profit from the millennium bug.*

Already, certain businesses are profiting from the computer glitch, such as emergency food suppliers, precious metals dealers, computer programmers, generator manufacturers, water purification companies, and canning and packaging supply companies. As the millennium bug continues to munch its way through our society, you should try remain alert for opportunities that you can profit from. Doing so will supplement your income and add stability to your household.

What opportunities actually arise will be dictated by the severity of Y2K on our communities. For instance, if there is an extended blackout, you could profit from selling candles, matches, lamp oil wicks, et cetera that people would need to light their homes. All you would have to do is stockpile these items now and then market your business after the lights go out. Another opportunity presented by a blackout is generator repair. You could get your training today, in anticipation of making money fixing generators in 2000.

Other businesses that may profit from Y2K include:

temporary employment services (e.g., bookkeepers, accountants)
Y2K assessment and repair services
child-care services
carpentry
engine repair
hunting and fishing supplies
security guard services
courier services
blacksmithing
warehousing
auctioneers
gunsmithing
flea markets
bicycle repair
tailor/sewing services
medical, dental, and veterinary services
teaching/tutoring
well-drilling services
welding services
plumbing services
gardening

used car sales
farmer's markets
midwifery
auto repair

You should also be aware that as discretionary income wallows in a declining economy, certain businesses will be hard hit. This includes retail, restaurants, real estate, new car sales, banking, landscaping, high technology, and the service industry (e.g., ad agency, printing).

TIP ▶ 81 *Buy real estate at the height of Y2K.*

There is one last way you can profit from Y2K. If it triggers a recession or depression, then there will be a number of home foreclosures. (People who lose their jobs will eventually be unable to make their monthly mortgage payments if they do not find employment.)

If you are financially able to do so, it would be wise to purchase real estate during this time when property values and loan interest rates will be at their lowest. You will be able to buy much more land and a larger house than you could ever imagine. This buyers market will be a boon to first-time home-owners and for new-home construction. So take advantage of it—you may never have a chance like it again in your lifetime.

Special Considerations

IT IS EASY TO OVERLOOK THE OBVIOUS

> The public faces a risk that critical services provided by the government and the private sector could be severely disrupted by the year 2000 computing problem. Financial transactions could be delayed, flights grounded, power lost, and national defense affected.
> —GAO Report
> January 20, 1999

As you continue your preparation efforts for Y2K, you may overlook some of the more obvious tasks, such as debugging your home computer or making preparations for an elderly parent. This chapter serves as an oh-by-the-way reminder for you. It covers a variety of obvious (and not-so-obvious) issues that you need to consider and take action on.

TIP 82 *Assess your PC for Y2K problems.*

There are 154 million personal computers hidden away in homes and office cubicles across America. If you own one of them, you need to make it Y2K compliant. This includes computers that were made as recently as 1998! A survey done by Greenwich Mean Time on the impact of Y2K on PCs revealed that 93 percent of all PCs made before 1997 and 47 percent of all PCs made in 1997 *and later* will produce incorrect dates when the year 2000 arrives. This is why you cannot assume your home computer is okay, even if you only use it to send E-mails to friends. Y2K pertains to you, like it or not.

And not only do you have to inspect your PC, but also your computer monitor, printer, software programs, data files, external disk storage, sound card, modems, graphics card, scanner, digital camera and keyboard. They are all warm, cozy hiding places for Y2K.

In any computer, there are three areas involved with time-keeping, which is where the millennium bug could exist:

Real-Time Clock (RTC)—This is a running clock that keeps track of the two-digit year value (e.g., 99 in 1999). Since it works when the computer is on or off, it is independently powered by a battery.

Complementary Metal Oxide Semiconductor (CMOS)—A memory chip that stores the RTC data. It works when the computer is turned off.

Basic Input-Output System (BIOS)—This serves as the middleman between your computer hardware and the operating system (OS). It works when the computer is turned on or off.

Whenever you turn on your computer, the operating system (e.g., Windows, DOS) immediately requests the date and time. BIOS receives this message and then goes to get the information from the real-time clock. It passes the date and time on to the operating system, which then keeps a running clock

---

CLUES THAT YOU MAY HAVE A Y2K PROBLEM

- You are using an old version of the software.
- The vendor is no longer in business.
- The program was specially written or modified for you.
- Your computer was put together in a friend's garage.
- The software only runs on DOS.
- Your computer has a 486, 386 or earlier Pentium processor chip.
- Software or hardware is no longer supported.
- Your software programs are either freeware or shareware, and you can't locate the author or current information on it.
- You have made a lot of modifications to the program.
- Calendar functions will not allow you to see past 1999.

Source: Senator John F. Kerry (D-MA)
www.senate.gov/~Kerry/isy2k.htm

of its own. It is this clock that your applications (e.g., spreadsheets, accounting, word processing) use when booted up.

Along this chain, the most likely place for a Y2K error is in BIOS since many were programmed to accept dates only between January 1, 1980 and December 31, 1999. Thus, what your computer needs is a "patch"—a quasi-computer Band-Aid—to allow BIOS to recognize dates 2000 and beyond. Fortunately, many computer manufacturers (but not all!) have already identified whether or not their BIOS is okay and, if not, have created patches you can use.

So your first step in assessing your computer for Y2K problems is to call your computer manufacturer and inquire about BIOS. You can also do this by visiting their Web site, if they have one. (See Appendix 3 for a listing of computer Web sites.)

Another option is to visit www.nstl.com and use the free analysis program to test your BIOS, or visit www.rightime.com and download their program, "Test2000.zip."

Once you have determined whether or not your computer's BIOS is safe, you then have to assess all the software you use. The applications that are most likely to have a Y2K problem include:

- databases and spreadsheets
- accounting, financial, and tax software
- project-management programs
- antivirus software
- fax and E-mail programs

Again, you call your software manufacturer directly or visit their Web site to learn of any Y2K problems they have discovered. Oftentimes, patches are made available on their Web site.

Good Internet sites you should know about for PC and software testing, include:

software patches	www.year2000.com/y2klinks.html
ZDNet	www.zdnet.com/vlabs/y2k/testy2k.html
PC testing tool	www.pcprofile.com
year 2000 testing	www.year2000.com/y2klinks.html

If you do not want to do the Y2K testing yourself, then consider buying a commercial software program. These generally analyze not only your BIOS but also your applications, and fix them. Some of the more popular programs include:

Y2000RTC Fix, $40 (Micro Star)
  800-777-4228,
    www.microstar-usa.com or www.y2000rtc.com
2000 Toolbox, $29 (Network Associates)
  888-712-1477, www.mcafee.com
Norton 2000, $49 (Symantec Corp.)
  800-441-7234, www.symantec.com/sabu/n2000r
Fix2000 Pro, $50 (Intelliquis)
  801-553-1127, www.intelliquis.com/sitemap.html
Prove It 2000, $47 (Davis Gates Smith)
  877-748-2020, www.proveit2000usa.com

A word of warning! No matter what you do, do *not* set your computer system clock ahead to just before midnight on December 31, 1999 to see how the computer behaves as it rolls over to the year 2000. This may sound like a logical thing to do, but it can result in problems with your existing programs and data. Besides, even if your computer passes the test, you could still have date-related errors with the BIOS because the test is not complete. If, for some reason, you still feel compelled to do it, make a complete backup of your hard drive before running the test. Also, print out any crucial reports, such as account balances from any personal finance program.

▶ TIP 83 *If you own a Macintosh, test it for Y2K problems.*

In spite of what you have heard, even Macintosh computers must be assessed for Y2K. Although there are generally no Mac hardware and operating system problems—Apple has been using the four-digit date since the mid-1980s—you do need to be concerned about the *software applications* you run on your computer. Many programs have Y2K problems, which will be affected when January 1, 2000 rolls around. So call your software manufacturers or visit their Web sites to learn of any glitches and to get the patches necessary to fix them.

Also, visit Apple's Web site to make absolutely certain that there are no hardware problems with your computer. Apple has tested all of its products—from printers to cameras, and from keyboards to monitors—and posted the results at: www.apple.com/about/year2000/y2khwtests.html

▶ TIP 84 *Avoid recontaminating your computer with the millennium bug.*

Once you have ensured that your computer is free of Y2K problems, don't allow the bug to return. You can do this by not downloading documents/data from suspected or known "dirty" sources (stop using shareware), and by purchasing software that specifically states it is Y2K compliant.

Additionally, before adding any new peripherals to your system—such as a scanner, zip drive, or printer—do some investigative footwork and make sure that it does not have a Y2K problem. Visit Electronic Data Systems's Web site (www.eds. com) and search its database of 125,000 hardware and software products to learn if they are year 2000 compliant.

▶ TIP 85 *Test for leap year!*

The year 2000 is unusual in that it is not only the end of the century, but it is also a leap year. This combination occurs once every 400 years. Because of this, many computer operating systems, BIOS chips, and computer applications were not programmed for it. Hence, you need to make certain that they will recognize February 29, 2000. Many of the Y2K-test software programs mentioned in Tip 82 do check for this compatibility.

If you absolutely have to do this test yourself—without the

use of commercial software—simply reset the date and time on your computer to 11:59 p.m. on 02-28-2000. However, remember to back up your hard drive first, just in case the system crashes!

▶ TIP 86 *Reset electronic devices to 1972.*

You probably own a number of electronic devices in your home that have embedded systems or use a date-sensitive chip. Examples include:

- Digital camera
- Video camera
- Camera multifunction back (35mm)
- VCR
- Fax machine
- Television
- Printers
- Clock radios
- Handheld organizers
- CD players
- Digital watches

If you are able to do so, as in the case of most cameras and VCRs, reprogram the device's date on January 1, 2000 to January 1, 1972. That year's calendar dates and days of the week are identical to the year 2000, including the leap year date of February 29.

▶ TIP 87 *Back up tax and banking software programs.*

All tax and banking software programs—Quicken, MacInTax, and TurboTax to name a few—rely on date calculations to determine interest rates, stock gains, amortization schedules, et cetera. Because of this, they are at high risk for Y2K problems.

If you have not done so already, call the manufacturer of your tax or banking software (or, visit their Internet Web site), and inquire if a patch is needed to correct any Y2K glitches.

As a precaution, you should back up all your data files—bank accounts, investment files, household budget, autopayment programs—on a disk and make hard copies of crucial accounts.

TIP ⑧⑧ *Protect your home business*.

More people operate a business out of their home today than ever before, often using computers to get the work done. Yet, surprisingly, according to the Small Business Administration, very few home-based businesses have taken steps to protect themselves from Y2K disruptions. Why is this?

Many wrongly believe that Y2K is a big-computer problem, such as mainframes and business network computers. They fail to understand that the PC is equally vulnerable.

Another reason is that small business owners do not grasp the domino effect that Y2K could have on their business, even if it does not strike their own systems. For instance, slow payment from customers as a result of a Y2K glitch affecting either the postal service or banking system could place their business in jeopardy by throwing its cash flow out of balance. This, in turn, could result in the inability to pay staff, delays in accounts payable (thereby affecting the company's credit rating), and a slowdown in production (inability to purchase raw materials).

If you operate a business, even if you do not use a computer, you must sit down and determine how Y2K could potentially affect your sales, inventory, supplies, and raw materials, and cash flow. For example, if you make jam at home for sale in grocery stores, here are just a few of the issues you would need to think about:

- Are your suppliers of canning jars, boxes, labels, fruit, and gelling agents Y2K compliant? Can they guarantee you a steady supply so you can meet your delivery obligations and cash flow requirements?
- Could there ever be a delay in getting the jars to you?
- If you are late in getting the jam to the distributor, will you be fined or held liable for breach of contract for failing to deliver the product as initially agreed upon?
- Will your insurance company cover Y2K-induced damages? For example, if there is a blackout one winter's night and your jams freeze, thereby causing the jars to shatter, will you be reimbursed for the loss?
- Will you be able to ship your jam to your distributor(s) without any delays?
- Will the distributor(s) be able to get your jams out to the grocery stores?
- If there is a slowdown in accounts receivable (or if the electronic bank deposit system crashes), how long can you survive financially? How will you pay your vendors?

As is apparent, Y2K could easily bring this home-based jam business to its knees . . . even though the owner does not have a computer!

So how do you protect your business? 1) Ensure that your computers and software programs are Y2K compliant (see Tip 82); 2) talk with your vendors and suppliers to make certain that they have taken proper and aggressive steps to be Y2K compliant and, if they have not, to consider changing vendors; 3) back up on disk and print out on paper all crucial records needed by your business to survive (e.g., bookkeeping, client files, databases, spreadsheets); 4) find out what your insurance policy will and will not cover, and then take steps to minimize the effects of the noncovered possibilities; 5) examine and test all digital office equipment to find out which ones are not Y2K compliant and then either fix or replace them; 6) determine what your legal liabilities could be if Y2K prevents you from fulfilling a contractual obligation, and talk with an attorney about how to minimize this threat.

TIP 89 *Consider the special needs of the disabled and elderly.*

In our busy and hectic world, it is very easy, when preparing for Y2K, to overlook the special needs of elderly parents and of those of any age who are disabled. Yet we need to stop a moment and consider Y2K from their point of view, for it can present unique and challenging issues.

For instance, if a loved one relies on a stair elevator to get to the second floor, how will he or she do so if the power goes out? Or if someone uses a battery-powered wheelchair, how will it be recharged? Or if someone is reliant on a medical device (e.g., home dialysis, life support), is it Y2K compliant?

These and many other issues must be addressed, and solutions found. Here, then, are some tips for you to follow:

- Have a copy of eyeglass prescriptions.
- Have a list of medications and their dosage.
- Stockpile food that meets the individual's special dietary needs.
- If a service dog is used, make certain that its food and water requirements will be met. Also, have the dog's ID tag, vaccination record, veterinary record, and any medications it needs.
- Have extra batteries for hearing aids, medical devices, and battery-operated wheelchairs and carts.
- Collect and safeguard the following documents: will, power of attorney, medical power of attorney, advanced directives, prescriptions, medical and dental records, health insurance policy, and health-care card.
- On a sheet of paper, record the name and phone numbers of the following: physician, dentist, therapist, hospital, attorney, and ambulance service.
- Ensure that all medical devices being used are Y2K com-

pliant. To find out, ask the physician, call the manufacturer, or visit one of the following Internet Web sites:
www.fda.gov
www.medical-devices.gov.uk
www.shef.ac.uk/uni/projects/hij/y2kdef2.htm
www.fda.gov/cdrh *(radiological devices)*

- If your loved one relies on power to stay alive (e.g., life-
support equipment), call your utility company and request that you be placed on their list for priority recon-
nection service.
- Identify fire exits in the home that the elderly and/or disabled can easily and quickly use.

A few last thoughts: if an elderly parent or a disabled loved
one lives alone, consider inviting them to stay with you when
Y2K strikes. This is especially necessary if there is a blackout
or if the food distribution system collapses. They could be vic-
timized by criminals, who will consider them, because of their
age or disability, to be easy targets for food, water and supplies.

And last, if you have an elderly parent or neighbor who
lived through the 1920s or 1930s, ask for their advice about
preparedness. Having endured the Great Depression, they
know what it is like to struggle to survive.

TIP ⑨⓪ *Don't overlook your pets.*

You need to make sure your pet is ready for the millennium bug's bite. For instance, stockpile a month's worth of
food and two weeks of water for them. Also make sure you
have an adequate supply of medications or supplements they
might need. Talk with your vet and put together a first-aid kit
you can use to treat your pet in emergencies.

As for cats and dogs, see to it that they are up-to-date on
their vaccinations and that you have a copy of their veterinary
records and rabies tags. It is also a good idea to have a current

color photograph of Fido and Ms. Molly in case they run off and get lost. It will help in the search effort.

Fish, especially tropical fish, pose a distinct problem since they rely on heated water to stay alive. If the power goes out and the water temperature drops, even a few degrees, they could die. So if you own exotic fish, you need to find a way to keep the water at a proper temperature. Talk with your pet store to learn about heating options.

And last, if you own birds, be aware that fumes from a kerosene or propane heater, as well as from a burning lamp or scented candle, can critically injure a bird. So be alert for signs that the bird is being overcome (e.g., wobbliness, open beak, closed eyes).

TIP 91 *Prepare your children for the millennium bug.*

Children are surprisingly knowledgeable about Y2K: they watch television shows and are intimately familiar with computers and handheld electronic toys. Because of this, do not hide Y2K issues from them. As mentioned earlier, get them involved in your preparation efforts right from the start. Doing so will lower their stress and keep them informed about what is going on.

A variety of government agencies have recognized this fact and have either produced documents or created special Internet Web sites just for children. (The CIA has even published a Y2K coloring book for children!) Four of the more popular sites are:

Y2K for Kids	www.y2kculture.com/reactions/ 19990218.kids.html
2000Now Kids	www.2000now.org/kids.htm
Australia Kids	www.2000aware.com/Education/ Kids/kids.html
FEMA for Kids	www.fema.gov/kids

HELPING YOUR CHILD COPE WITH Y2K

Many parents instinctively ban painful topics from family conversations—and Y2K is certainly a painful topic. However, such a strategy can intensify a child's despair and negativity. Most children are quite sensitive and look to their parents and older siblings for clues about how to react to a particular situation. Thus, if you are alarmed, your child may become more frightened. He sees your anxiety as proof that the danger is real.

Children fear four things: death (of a loved one); darkness, abandonment, and animals. They also become quite anxious when their daily routine is upset.

To alleviate these fears, sit down and talk with your children. Acknowledge their fears and reassure them with firmness and love. Oftentimes according to psychologists, a simple statement like "We are together. We care about you. We will take care of you." is enough to wipe the anxiety away . . . temporarily, that is. It is not unusual for children to need reassurance many times. So you may find yourself repeating the same information and reassurances over and over again. Just be patient.

Also, provide comfort by holding, hugging, and kissing your children. Close physical contact reinforces in your children's minds the fact that you are there and will not abandon them.

If you begin to see symptoms of stress (see Tip #94) in your children, talk with them about their feelings: Are they angry? Sad? If so, about what? At a difficult time such as this, you should seek the advice of a clergy member or mental health professional, especially if the fear, anger or depression seems to be lingering and becoming worse.

TIP 92 *Be ready for an extended "school holiday."*

There is a chance that America's school system will be out of operation as a result of Y2K problems. Why? A poll conducted by the National Association of Counties in November 1998 showed that local governments, which includes the school system, are poorly prepared for Y2K. Half the counties surveyed had no plan in place to deal with Y2K. Exacerbating this is the fact that schools themselves have neither the money nor the on-staff ability to handle and rectify Y2K's technical aspects. Because of this, children are likely to have an extended Christmas holiday in 1999. This is especially true if there is a power outage, since schools need heat, lighting, and running water to function.

Unfortunately, if Y2K does wreak havoc across the country, America will have its hands full restoring vital functions and services, such as hospital care. Education will be at the bottom of the list because it is not required for survival. So you may have your children hanging around the home for a while until the Y2K mess is straightened out.

Although the children will not necessarily mind this, you should. It is important to keep them on track with their educational learning. Hence, you need to give some consideration to the prospect of home schooling. Call your child's school and inquire about the laws and school-board regulations governing home schooling in your state. If a suggested curriculum is available, get your hands on it.

The school may also be able to recommend an accredited home-schooling program to you. There are a number of programs available, and it can be confusing to figure out which one to follow. (See Appendix 2.)

If you want to learn more about home schooling, contact *Home Education Magazine* (800-236-3278, www.home-ed-press.com). They are a fantastic source of information about how to set up a home-schooling program, state laws and regulations, accredited home-school programs, and resources for books and teaching supplies.

Should you elect not to pursue the home-schooling option, you should still visit your child's school and get copies of his or her transcripts and any crucial test results (e.g., PSAT, IQ, SAT, GRE).

For children who receive special services (e.g., speech therapy), you need to get copies of progress reports, diagnostic evaluations, and education plans.

As for high school juniors and seniors, they should retain copies of all college applications (especially if the application was submitted via computer) and student financial aid forms.

▶ TIP 93 *Find alternate forms of entertainment.*

A life without electricity means a life without television, stereos, VCRs, and computer games. Even if you purchase a generator, you will be limiting your electronic pleasures to perhaps an hour or two a day. That means there will likely be unhappy campers scattered all over the house, bored out of their minds.

This is perhaps the best and least-anticipated benefit of Y2K: it will force family members to interact with one another again as they should. Instead of children sitting zombielike in front of the television set for seven hours a day, they will talk and play with their siblings, friends, and parents. As a result, the core family bond will be strengthened. Essentially, we will be turning the clock back to an era when the family came first before anything else.

To encourage family interaction and to preserve your own sanity if Y2K drags on, make sure you find alternate forms of entertainment, such as board games, crossword puzzles, books, and arts and crafts. For the rare treat, buy handheld electronic games than operate on one or two double-A batteries. (Consider using Ni-Cad batteries that can be recharged by a solar-powered battery charger.) If you or anyone else in the family has ever wanted to pursue a particular hobby, the Y2K downtime is a good time to do it. Buy the materials you will need ahead of time.

▶ TIP 94 *Know how to recognize and deal with stress and depression.*

When I first got tuned in to this "monuMENTAL monster," I was depressed for two weeks; I was going through ink and paper with my printer like crazy. I was making myself crazy and my husband thought I was crazy. I have read everything I could find and heard all I could hear on Y2K. Everything from the government conspiracy to just the bump in the road; the best scenario to the worst scenario. I have been through the emotional ups and downs of it all, and will probably continue to go back and forth. . . .

As this letter from "Anna of Florida" suggests, Y2K is an ugly topic that can instill anxiety in people when they sit back and think about all the disastrous scenarios that could occur. As you and your family go about preparing for Y2K-related problems—and later, if you actually experience blackouts and food shortages—stress and depression could settle in. That is a natural response. The problem arises when this anxiety, fear, and sadness remain and begin to adversely affect your physical health and mental well-being.

Stress manifests itself in many different ways, which is why

Y2K ANXIETY DAY . . . DECEMBER 1, 1999

Feeling a bit uptight about preparing for the millennium bug? Concerned by how it could affect your life? Well, you can rest easier now because on December 1, 1999 counselors will be donating their time to help alleviate your fear. All you have to do is call 1–800-THERAPIST (1–800–843–7274) and a therapist will answer your questions and provide anxiety-reducing suggestions.

If you have access to the Internet, there will an on-line chat forum in which you can see a therapist live and have E-mail questions answered while you watch. The address is www.1–800-therapist.com/Y2K.html

In the meanwhile, you can request a free brochure, *"Ten Steps to Handling Y2K Anxiety,"* by sending a self-addressed, stamped envelope to:

1–800-Therapist Network
2923 Camino del Mar, No. 6
Del Mar, CA 92014

it can be initially difficult to detect. Oftentimes we simply ignore the signs, attributing them to something else. Some of the more common symptoms include:

Psychological and Emotional
anxiety
irritability
moodiness, crying, depression
anger, blaming
diminished interest in usual activities
feelings of isolation
denial
recurring nightmares about potential or real Y2K disasters
inability to fall asleep, or remain asleep
sleeping excessively

Mental
poor concentration
mental confusion
forgetfulness
inability to make decisions
unable to prioritize tasks
unable to express yourself verbally or in writing

Physical
headache
nausea
sweating or chills
numbness in a part of the body
chest pain
fatigue
heart palpitations
shaking
rapid breathing
muscle soreness

Behavior
outburst of anger
frequent arguments

not able to be objective
increased use of alcohol, tobacco, or other drugs
withdrawal from people

No one is immune from depression's grasp. In any given six months, 9 million Americans—adults and children—suffer from a depression. (Females are more susceptible to depression than males.) It interferes with normal day-to-day functioning and causes suffering not only to those who have a disorder but also to those who care about them. In some instances, serious depression can destroy family life. It can also influence some ill people to commit suicide.

If you can, try to maintain a positive attitude as you prepare for and endure the millennium bug, even when things become difficult. (See "Y2K Anxiety Day . . . December 1, 1999" on page 180.) There are a number of techniques that you can use to reduce your anxiety, such as deep breathing, yoga, meditation, and relaxation exercises. You can learn more about stress relief by reading *The Book of Stress Survival: Identifying and Reducing the Stress in Your Life* by Alix Kirsta.

If someone in your family is diagnosed as being depressed, you can support him or her in the following ways:

- Try to maintain as normal a relationship as possible.
- Do not expect him or her to "snap out of it."
- Express your affection and support.
- Keep him or her actively involved in family activities.
- Do not criticize or blame his/her depressive behavior.
- Avoid saying things that might worsen his/her poor self-image.

TIP 95 *Consider leaving the city.*

This, admittedly, is a drastic step to take. Not everyone will agree with the idea of selling your home (or vacating an apartment) and relocating to a rural town. But for some people, the strategy has merit, which is why it is included here.

As you have probably noticed so far reading this book, Y2K

is going to affect cities and rural communities quite differently. Of the two, cities stand to suffer the most. They are also the most difficult environments for a person to survive a disaster in.

Why? Because without electricity, you will have thousands of people stuck in high-rise buildings with no elevators, running water, or heat. Even if people want to weather Y2K by preparing for it, there is limited storage space for food and water stockpiles. There is also little space to grow a vegetable garden or raise animals.

Additionally, people are limited in the alternate heating sources they can use. Woodstoves and gas stoves are usually out of the question since: 1) you cannot install a chimney on the 12th floor of a 20-story building, and 2) there is no place to store 5 to 10 cords of wood or a 250-gallon propane tank.

Furthermore, unless a city is located on a lake or has a river running through it, there are few if any emergency water sources.

And last, cities generally have gangs and an underclass, both of which could prey on the rich to acquire the food, water, and shelter they need to survive. City streets could be paved with death and danger.

This reality is understood by many people, including the following anonymous engineer, who sent an E-mail to Internet columnist Roleigh Martin: "*I do not plan to be anywhere near a big (or medium) city when the year 2000 hits. There is just too much that could go wrong.*"

If you live in the city, you may want to give serious thought to moving to the countryside. Many people have done so in recent years—states like Wyoming, Montana, Arizona, New Mexico, and Colorado have seen a tremendous influx of new residents. These people are not necessarily relocating because of Y2K, mind you, but rather because they want to escape the rat race and live in an environment where family and community still mean something.

Depending on your feelings about Y2K, you may want to relocate. If you do decide to move, do it before the economy crashes so you can sell your property at a profit. You also want to move before winter sets in so you can make necessary preparations at your new home, such as stacking wood, winterizing the house, and putting up canned goods.

Realize that moving to the country does not make you immune from Y2K—it will still bite rural towns. The difference is that a rural environment gives you more options for water, food, and self-sufficiency. For instance, there are likely to be ponds and streams nearby. There will be more land available to grow crops and raise animals on. There will be areas where you can hunt deer and small game. And there will be more opportunities for you to harness the sun, wind, or water to generate electricity.

But this not to suggest that rural life has no drawbacks. The two largest issues where Y2K is concerned are: 1) employment, and 2) restoration of services. If the economy goes sour, small towns are typically harder hit than an urban area. So if you lose your job, you may be out of work for a long time.

As for restoration of services, governments at all levels— federal, state, and local—always give priority to regions with the greatest number of people. For instance, a city of 100,000 people will get its power back far quicker than a town of 1,200. So if you move out to the country and become a victim of Y2K, expect to be among the last to get your electricity and grocery store goods.

CHECK IT OUT . . . YOURSELF

Small business
   www.sba.gov/y2k
   www.score.org/y2k
   www.vendor2000.com

Computer testing
   dir.yahoo.com/ComputersandInternet/Year2000Problem
   www.pcmag.com/y2k
   www.willitwork.com

Elderly and disabled
   www.redcross.org/disaster/safety/disability.html
   www.aarp.org

Pets
   www.fema.gov/fema/anemer.htm
   www.redcross.org/disaster/safety/pets.html

Home schooling
   American Homeschool Association
      www.home-ed-magazine.com/AHA/aha.html
   Alliance for Parental Involvement in Education
      www.croton.com/allpie
   Catholic Homeschool Network of America
      home.att.net/~harryl
   Jewish Home Educator's Network
      jhen@snj.com
   National Homeschool Association
      www.n-h-a.org
   The Adventist Home Educator
      www.adventtech.com/ahe

Y2K real estate exchange
   www.y2ksurvive.com/property.html

Reaching Out to Others

WE CANNOT AFFORD TO BE COMPLACENT

Each day I am more alarmed and dismayed: alarmed at the potential chaos, and dismayed at the "business as usual" atmosphere. The more I learn (about Y2K), the more concerned I am.
—Cindy (New Hampshire)

May you live in interesting times."

Whoever uttered this statement obviously had other things in mind: medical progress, for instance. Or, perhaps, discovering life elsewhere in the universe. Anything but a computer programming glitch—and an embarrassingly simple one at that!

People usually do not like hearing or receiving bad news, especially if it affects them, which is why many have turned their backs on Y2K. They find it absurd to believe that the omission of "19" from a computer program could possibly bring society to its knees. But that indeed is the reality confronting us, not only here in America but in nations around the globe.

You have a responsibility to share your knowledge about Y2K with your family, friends, and loved ones. They may not accept it at first, but that does not mean they should not be informed.

This chapter shows you how to communicate with others about Y2K, and the importance of doing so. It will not be an easy task. In fact, it could be quite difficult since some people you care about will ridicule or dismiss you.

That is to be expected, and you should not take their actions to heart. Remember that at one time you, too, were freaked

---

WHO SAYS Y2K ISN'T FUNNY?

MEMO
TO: *Business Manager*
FROM: *Information Systems*

  I hope I haven't misunderstood your instructions. Because, to be honest, none of this Y to K problem makes any sense to me.
  At any rate, I have finished converting all the months on all the company calendars so that the year 2000 is ready to go with the following new months and weekdays:

Januark
Februark
Mak
Julk
Mondak
Tuesdak
Wednesdak
Thursdak
Fridak
Saturdak
Sundak

---

out about the millennium bug before you finally acknowledged the danger it posed to you and your family. So give them time.

TIP 96 *Make sure your community is preparing for Y2K.*

Disaster can bring out the best in people: they unite to overcome the adversity that has befallen their fellow man. Entire communities, for instance, often rally to assist those who have lost their homes and belongings to fires, floods, hurricanes, tornadoes, and earthquakes. Strangers show up from nowhere and generously provide food, shelter, and even cash out of their pockets to help the unfortunate get back on their feet.

Not a day goes by without us hearing a warmhearted story on television about someone reaching out to another with concern and charity. This behavior is innate, and it is the mortar that binds us together.

Y2K is a technological disaster that will arrive in full force on January 1, 2000. At this point no one really knows how bad it will be, but we do know that it *will* impact our lives since Y2K-related incidents are already occurring. Just as we prepare for an impending natural disaster so, too, must we come together as a community to prepare for this technological storm and, once it strikes, to clean up the mess and get our lives back on track.

It is disheartening to realize that many towns, cities, and counties across the nation have not taken any preventive actions to date. Instead, they are taking a respond-on-failure stance. It is an approach that will prove to be expensive and ineffectual.

This is where you come into the picture. Contact your town or city officials and ask what has been done prepare for Y2K. If nothing has been done, demand to know why when it is crystal clear to even the federal government that preparations need to be made. If assessment steps have been taken, ask where they stand in fixing Y2K problems and then testing them. Oftentimes you will find that a city has completed its assessment of the problem, but has made very little progress in fixing them, owing to the expense and time limitations.

Similarly, ask if a contingency plan has been developed to maintain or restore vital services to the community. Is the plan in writing? (If so, can you receive a copy of it?) Has the plan been approved by the major or board of selectman? More importantly, have any drills been undertaken to actually test the plan to make sure it works and that nothing has been overlooked?

And last, ask if any public meetings are scheduled to be held to inform residents about what they should (or should not) be doing. If not, why not? After all, don't residents—the same ones who vote public officials into office and who pay city taxes and employee salaries—have a right to know what is being done about Y2K?

If you find that your public officials refuse to cooperate with you by answering these simple questions, consider contacting a local newpaper or television station. Explain your experience to a reporter, and encourage him or her to investigate the story. Since elected officials refused to be open with you, it will make the reporter suspicious that there is a cover-up going on. Your phone call or visit will spur action.

TIP 97 *Organize a neighborhood Y2K meeting.*

"There is safety in numbers." This axiom survives because it has proven itself true over the centuries; you should heed its wisdom when making preparations for Y2K. One person or a single family, with restricted financial resources and skills, can only accomplish so much, but a group of people working together in an organized manner can achieve greater feats.

This is why the popular neighborhood watch works so well in urban areas. A network of volunteers in each neighborhood keeps an eye out for suspicous-acting people and reports drug deals and other crimes to the police. This keeps the neighborhood free of criminals and preserves the quality of life found in the area.

Consider taking a similar approach in your Y2K preparation efforts. The benefits of a joint neighborhood effort are numerous:

- It provides safety, since everyone looks out for one another and unites if difficulties present themselves.
- You are able to identify skills and resources that the group as a whole can benefit from, such as having a nurse in the neighborhood to provide first-aid services in an emergency.
- You can pool your stockpiling efforts. Everyone pitches

in to make sure there are adequate supplies for any Y2K contingency.

- It provides for cross-training opportunities. For instance, everyone can learn gardening skills from a neighbor who has formal training or extensive experience in this area.
- It offers mental-health relief. You are no longer alone in your Y2K preparation efforts. You have people to talk with to alleviate your stress and anxiety.

There are two ways to organize a Y2K meeting: you can invite everyone over for a potluck dinner, or visit with each family one-on-one. Which option you choose depends on your comfort talking in front of a group of people—the most common phobia.

Regardless of how you approach it, you will still need to organize your thoughts. A very simple agenda to follow would be:

1. Explain what Y2K is, including the embedded chip problem.
2. Discuss how Y2K could disrupt services. Give examples of how Y2K-related problems are already happening. Get feedback from people as to what things they fear could happen.
3. Explain what preparation efforts have been suggested by the Red Cross, the government, and various Y2K experts.
4. Ask people to think about the prospect of uniting together to make preparations for Y2K more cost effective.

Before the meeting, prepare a fact sheet about the millennium bug that you can hand out to everyone. It should include basic things like the federal government's Y2K hotline number, a list of Web sites that people can browse through at their leisure, a copy of Senator Moynihan's letter to President Clinton, and a copy of the June 2, 1997 *Newsweek* cover story. (Making a copy of this book available for people to flip through may be helpful as well.)

Also, have a list of factual bullets about Y2K. Not doomsayer speculations, but *hardcore facts* from sources that no one can dispute. Feel free to use the following examples, which come from official government reports, press releases and filed newswire stories:

- The federal government is encouraging families to have $500 cash on hand for Y2K-related emergencies.
- The American Red Cross is advocating that families stockpile a week's worth of emergency food. (A U.S. Senate report endorses this as well: "Stockpiling a small amount of extra food and water in the event of temporary shortages may also be advisable.")
- The General Accounting Office has stated that the federal government needs to do more than it has to be Y2K compliant by the end of 1999.
- Social Security may be Y2K compliant, but the agency that cuts the checks—the Financial Management Service—is *not*, and is not expected to be by December 31, 1999. FMS handles financial transactions for almost every government agency, including IRS refunds and military retirement payments.
- The Securities and Exchange Commission has fined dozens of companies for refusing to disclose their preparations for Y2K.
- Many states are gearing up their National Guard units for possible deployment at the end of 1999 to handle riots and looting.
- After learning that their payroll computer was not Y2K compliant, Congress unanimously voted in February 1999 to buy a new $770,000 system to ensure that they receive their paychecks. (Ironically, congressional aides get their paychecks from a different system, and it is *not* Y2K compliant.)
- The Nuclear Regulatory Commission, at this writing, is deciding whether or not to order nuclear power plants to have generators and 60 days of fuel available as a safety precaution in case the power goes out.

- Michael Powell, the commissioner of the Federal Communications Commission, has said it's too late to squash the millennium bug. "We're definitely past the period of where you're going to solve the (Y2K) problem. We're into mitigation." December 8, 1998
- John Koskinen, the government's Y2K czar, has stated that he has no faith in railroads being Y2K compliant by December 31, 1999. This could affect the distribution of food products and industrial supplies nationwide.

During your presentation, you may lose a person or two after introducing Y2K as a looming problem. Why? Well, as the American poet and playwright T. S. Eliot put it, "Mankind cannot tolerate too much reality." Hence, some people will dismiss the problem entirely. That's fine. They are allowed to have their opinions. Don't waste your time trying to convince them otherwise. If they change their mind, they will find you.

The same holds true for those who seem to withdraw after hearing your news about Y2K. They may be retreating out of fear. They may wonder how modern technology could fail. Surely the government or a computer genius like Bill Gates will ride in on a white steed and fix things before it's too late, right? Again, respect their need to internalize and process the information; give them time and space—allow them to approach you.

Your role here is to serve as a sower of seeds. Plant the concern about Y2K and allow it to germinate. Sooner or later people will come to grips with the information and be able to address Y2K more bluntly.

Julie, who lives in Ohio, learned this lesson herself:

I've learned that trying to convince other people of the more serious implications of Y2K is a waste of time and energy. I will discuss, with caution, my own preparations and my reasons for preparing. I'll use any opening I can to impart information, answer questions, and try subtly to open minds to the possibilities. Many times, after a few days or a couple of weeks, I will hear from someone I've talked to. It might be a question, or a newspaper article in the mail, or a phone call. . . .

Once you have a few neighbors in agreement that a unified effort to prepare for Y2K is a good idea—it might take several meetings to reach this stage—you can proceed with the logistics. One of the first things you should do is take an inventory of what resources are available for joint use. This includes both physical resources (e.g., gardens, generators, radios, pools, woodstoves) and professional skills (e.g., carpentry, plumbing, medical, car repair, law enforcement, teacher).

From there, outline a plan on how you as a group will proceed in acquiring supplies and making preparations. Prioritize them and assign specific tasks, with deadlines, to each participant.

It may help your planning efforts if you candidly discuss the following questions and issues:

- How will you all communicate with each other? Will you, for instance, use CBs and walkie-talkies?
- What kind of security measures will you put in place? Will you patrol your neighborhood? If so, how? Who will lead this effort?
- Where will supplies be stockpiled? If they are divided up, how will you gain access to them? What kind of inventory system will you use? Who will oversee it?
- Will you establish child care? If so, where will it be located and who will operate it? Will you offer home schooling? Who will be your teachers? Where will you get curriculums, books, and teaching aids from?
- How many elderly and disabled people are there in the neighborhood? What special needs do they have? How will you integrate them into your community's preparation efforts?
- If someone is seriously injured, how will you handle it? Do you have the means of transporting the person to a hospital or nearby physician's office? Will you have someone in your neighborhood trained in advanced first aid?
- How will garbage be disposed of if trash collection is halted? Will you be able to recycle materials? If the sewer

system ceases to operate, how will you safely dispose of human waste?

- How will you fight a fire? Where will the tools be stored and who will be in charge of coordinating the effort?
- How will you light your homes at night? Will you share a generator, or simply designate a home or two for lighting?
- How will pets be cared for? Who will oversee their veterinary care? Similarly, if a wild or domestic animal wanders into your neighborhood, how will you deal with it?
- Will you have a communal garden? If so where, and who will tend it? What crops will you grow, and how will you harvest and preserve what you grow? By the same token, will you raise animals for food? If so, who will tend to their needs and who will butcher them?

This can be a tedious process, but it is a rewarding one. Anna, who lives in Florida, gathered her neighbors for a meeting on Y2K with great success:

> I have spoken at one church, have pulled together a neighborhood meeting, and have made many new friends whom God had put in my path. Several women and I get together and share information and pray about the situation. We all realize that each of us has our own special gifts—one knows how to research, another knows home canning, and another knows how to grind wheat and make bread.
>
> I am learning soap making, canning, candlemaking, dehydrating, dutch-oven cooking, jelly making and gardening and composting. What a wonderful life! I'm looking forward to the good old bartering days. . . .

Now Anna and her newfound friends are putting their skills to good use preparing their community for Y2K. It demonstrates that once again, there *is* strength in numbers.

TIP 98 *Avoid attracting desperate people.*

When Y2K strikes and leaves behind a swath of disruption in its wake, those individuals who were complacent and did not prepare in advance will find themselves struggling to survive. At some point they are going to be cold and hungry, and they are going to start searching for warmth and food.

If you are not careful, you may inadvertantly attract these desperate, and potentially dangerous, people to your home. How? By running your generator, having lights shining brightly, and by making noises associated with modern civilization.

Remember, in other people's minds, you are not supposed to have any of these things in a dark and quiet world. When people observe your prosperity, they may try to take it away for themselves.

This lesson was learned by many people living in New England and Canada in January 1998. A severe ice storm hit the region, layering the landscape in three inches of ice and knocking out electricity in some areas for a month. Thieves stole generators within minutes after their owners started them up. All the lowlifes had to do was listen for the distinctive puttering of the generator in the otherwise quiet environment. The sound was a homing beacon, leading people straight to the generator.

After a few thefts, people learned to chain their generators to the house or car. Others hid their generators inside sheds or basements, which had been soundproofed with jackets and old clothing.

To avoid problems, take the following precautions:

- Store your generator out of sight in a place where you can muffle the sound of the engine.
- If you generate electricity to run lights—off either a battery or generator—pull blackout drapes across your windows. The same holds true for white gas and propane lanterns.
- Maintain a low profile. Keep activities at your home to a minimum. A busy household attracts attention. (Remember how you found parties when in high school?)
- Blend in with the crowd. Don't wear brand-new clothes,

expensive jewelry, or anything that screams "I'm doing just fine, thank you." This includes bathing. When water is rationed, bathing is rationed. If you walk around clean as a whistle, it will attract people's attention. They will wonder what other valuables are stashed away with your water supply.

- Avoid cooking outdoors: the smell of grilled food may attract hungry people or animals.

- If it is at all possible, position your solar panels so they cannot be seen by passersby. It is a signal that says "We have power!" (The same holds true for windmills and watermills.)

- Dispose of your trash carefully. People do not need to know that you have an adequate supply of food and other necessities of life.

- Do not talk with anyone about the existence and/or extent your supplies. Word gets around . . . and eventually to the wrong person.

- Be careful displaying money or gold/silver coins. Handle transactions carefully so that people around you are not aware of your prosperity, regardless of how little it actually is. Make several small purchases instead of a single large one. You don't want rumors floating around that you are rich. That is how victims are made.

▶ T I P 99 *Test your Y2K preparedness plan.*

Planning is one thing, but doing is quite another. For example, you may have purchased a water filtration system, but have you actually grabbed a bucket, walked down to a pond, brought back five gallons of stagnant water and then tried to filter it?

Probably not. But you need to, so you know what to expect. In this instance, you may discover that hauling 40 pounds of water (that's what five gallons of water weighs!) is more strenuous than you originally thought, especially over long distances. You may also discover that the water filtration process is slower than what the manufacturer advertised, and that the purified water tastes flat and needs to be spruced up with flavoring. These are all good things to know now, before Y2K arrives.

Convince your family to go a few days without using electricity—a long weekend, perhaps. Use this as a test to see how well your preparedness plan actually works. Do everything you would do if the power were actually turned off: cook food on a camp stove, run the generator to operate appliances, take showers using a five-gallon bag, eat prepackaged food, et cetera. As you go through this test, be alert for problems.

When the test is complete, have a family meeting to discuss how well things went. Encourage everyone to make suggestions about how to fix problems. Identify items that need to be purchased. Figure out how to make processes run more efficiently. Then, with a to-do list in hand, get everything in order for the real event.

In the fall of 1999, pull out all your survival equipment, clean it up one last time, and make sure everything is in perfect working order. Read through the user's manuals to refresh your memory about the equipment's various features and how to properly (and safely!) operate it. This includes camping

---

CHECK IT OUT . . . YOURSELF

Neighborhood planning
    www.cassandraproject.org
    www.josephproject2000.org
    www.y2kwomen.com
    www.y2krecovery.com
    www.wild2k.com

Spiritual
    www.y2kprayershield.org

Y2K humor
    www.duh-2000.com

stoves, lanterns, generators, chain saws, vent-free propane heaters, et cetera.

TIP 100 *See the benefits of Y2K.*

Most of us acknowledge that Y2K, if left unimpeded, has the power to severely disrupt our lives. It is important, though, that we do not focus our attention solely on the negative aspects of Y2K, if for no other reason than to preserve our mental health! Y2K also presents a host of opportunities. Remember, every cloud has a silver lining, including digital storm clouds.

What are some of the benefits associated with Y2K? First, as mentioned in Chapter 8, it presents financial opportunities. If you have an entrepreneural spirit, you could do quite well in the millennium bug's destructive wake.

Second, Y2K is bringing families closer together, as well as uniting community members. People today have a much stronger sense of allegiance, altruism, and kindness. These are traits that have not been seen in quite some time. People are finally beginning to reject the selfish what's-in-it-for-me? approach to life.

Third, Y2K has forced people to get their household and financial affairs in order. (That's a miracle in itself!)

Fourth, Y2K has better prepared households to deal with natural disasters. If the bug wimps out, people will at least have food, water, and supplies on hand to deal with hurricanes, tornadoes, and earthquakes. Before Y2K, people talked about preparedness, but few actually did anything about it.

Fifth, Y2K has the potential to restructure government and the business world. Bureaucrats and business executives, for instance, have been forced to examine how various systems operate, and how services and products are delivered.

And last, Y2K has taught us that we can no longer depend so heavily (and blindly!) on technology. We must find balance in our lives and learn to be more self-sufficient. John, who lives in California, has come to understand this point:

> The one thing I have gotten the most out of all this is to realize just how much I was dependent on the system. After I realized this, I made certain changes to become less dependent on the system and I promised myself to never become that way again.
>
> If the grocery store closes, or if I lose my job, I don't want to be forced into an instant crisis over what to do. I want to be able to sit back and take my time thinking about things and not be under pressure because I don't have any food in the house and I have to feed my kids.
>
> In a way, it kind of makes me feel that maybe Y2K is a good thing. It has made me prioritize my life and it has caused me to make changes that I think are for the better.

TIP 101 *Remember, Y2K is about prudence, not panic.*

When it comes to predictions of how severely Y2K will disrupt society, there are two extremes. At the one end, absolutely nothing will happen, while at the other end, civilization comes to an end. Since Y2K problems are already occurring, we know that the "nothing" option is no longer viable. By the same token, since many companies and industries have taken successful steps to thwart Y2K, we know that teotwawki is also not a real possibility. That means Y2K's impact will be somewhere in between.

Acknowledging this, then, means all of us can take a calm and rational approach to preparing for Y2K. This is not to suggest, however, complacency! Action *must* be taken since December 31, 1999, is a deadline that cannot be changed; it is steadily approaching with each tick of the clock. But keep in mind that Y2K demands prudence, not panic. So prepare carefully and deliberately. Make a little progress each day instead of trying to get everything done in 24 hours.

As you go through this process, enjoy life and the feeling of calm, reassurance, and security you are creating for yourself and your family. You have, after all, been forewarned about Y2K and you are now making intelligent preparations in response. Just as your ancestors used to gather enough food and fuel a century ago to make it through the winter, so too are you making preparations to weather the approaching technological storm. If you are not severely affected by Y2K in the year 2000, then your efforts of today are not wasteful: you can maintain your supplies for a natural disaster, eat them, or even donate them to charity.

In the end, try to maintain a sense of humor. It is so easy to allow fear of the unknown to envelope us. When that happens, though, nothing is accomplished. Instead, force yourself to see the humor in Y2K, even when things become difficult. What humor is that? Well, one day you may receive the following letter in your mailbox. In fact, pray that you do. . . .

January 1, 2000
Re: Vacation Pay

Dear Valued Employee:

Our records indicate that you have not used any vacation time over the past 100 years. As I am sure you are aware, employees are granted three weeks of paid leave per year or pay in lieu of time off. One additional week is granted for every five years of service.

Please either take 9,400 days off work or notify our office and your next paycheck will reflect payment of $8,277,432.22, which will include all pay and interest for the past 1,200 months.

Sincerely,
Automated Payroll

Preparedness Budgets

Making preparations for Y2K requires that you purchase items you normally do not have at home, such as 30-gallon water drums. Since most people have limited financial resources to begin with, it can be difficult to figure out what to buy with those few precious dollars. What items are absolutely essential and which ones can you get by without?

To help you through this dilemma, three sample budgets have been pulled together. Priority is given to water, food and heat. It is assumed that you will use existing assets (e.g., clothing, cooking utensils) to keep warm and safe.

$500 Budget

30-gallon water container	$25*
oil lamp and oil	$50
nonvent heater	$150
20-pound Propane tank (one)	$25
propane fuel	$10
food	$240*

$1000 Budget

sleeping bag	$80*
oil lamp and oil	$50
30-gallon water container	$25*
nonvent heater	$150
20-pound Propane tank (two)	$50
propane	$20

*Cost will fluctuate depending on the number of people involved in the preparation effort.

food	$295*
first-aid kit	$30
used .38 special	$200
ammo	$100

$5000 Budget

generator (5,000 watt)	$1100
diesel (two-gallon/day for one mo.)	$200**
electrician (wire house)	$150
oil lamp and oil	$50
sleeping bag	$80*
30-gallon water container	$25*
woodstove	$1000
wood (three cords)	$375
food	$1240*
firearm	$300
ammo	$200
first-aid kit	$30
water purifier	$250

**Cost reflects the price of diesel fuel *and* the storage containers.

APPENDIX 2

Suppliers

$\mathbf{F}$inding a vendor to buy particular survival-related items from can be a time-consuming and frustrating experience at times. This listing, which is far from complete, is intended to help you get started with your initial search efforts. You will quickly notice that only a vendor's phone number and Internet Web site are listed. That is intentional—you do not have the luxury of time to correspond by "snail" mail to prepare for the millennium bug.

Please note that if a supplier specializes in a particular retail area, it is listed in parenthesis after the listing. And last, all Internet addresses are presumed to have **http://** typed before the actual address.

Desiccants and Oxygen Absorber Resources
American National Can Company, Chicago, IL, 312-399-3000
Eagle Can Company, Peabody, MA, 508-532-0400
Finger Lakes Packaging, Lyons, NY, 315-946-4826
Major Surplus & Survival, 800-441-8855,
    www.MajorSurplusNSurvival.com
Nitro-Pak Preparedness Center, 800-866-4876, www.nitro-pak.com
United Can Company, Hayward, CA, 510-881-4531
Walton Feed Inc., 800-847-0465, www.waltonfeed.com

Diatomaceous Earth Suppliers
All Gone! 800-373-3423 (Vero Beach, FL)
Fossil Shell Supply Co. 800-370-9920 (Amarillo, TX)
Eagle-Picher Minerals 800-663-5517 (Reno, NV)
Major Surplus & Survival, 800-441-8855,
    www.MajorSurplusNSurvival.com

Food Suppliers

Dehydrated camping food, MREs, gourmet foods, bulk food
   packages, et cetera
AlpineAire Foods, 800-322-6325, www.alpineaire.com
American Products Corp., 503-672-7502,
   www.americanfamilynetwork.com
Atlantic Spice Company, 800-316-7965, www.atlanticspice.com
B&A Products, 918-696-5998, www.baproducts.com
Cheaper Than Dirt, 888-625-3848, www.cheaperthandirt.com
Common Sense Products, 800-346-0368, www.npwt.net/~comsense
Country Store & Kitchen Specialties, 800-896-9131,
   www.HealthyHarvest.com
Emergency Essentials, 800-999-1863, www.beprepared.com
Food Storage Central, 503-585-0478, www.foodstorage.net/order
Future Foods, 800-949-FOOD
JRH Enterprises, 904-797-9462, www.logoplex.com/resources/jrh
Major Surplus & Survival, 800-441-8855, www.MajorSurplusN
   Survival.com
Maple Leaf Industries, 800-671-5323, www.mapleleafinc.com
Millennium Group, 800-500-9893, www.millenniumfoods.com
New Millennium Products, 910-799-7433
Nitro-Pak Preparedness Center, 800-866-4876, www.nitro-pak.com
Oregon Freeze Dry, 800-547-4060, www.ofd.com/mh
Perma-Pak Food Distributors, 888-495-FOOD, www.permapak.com
Preparedness Mart, 800-773-0437, www.preparednessmart.com
Preparedness Plus, 888-839-0334, www.enol.com~preplus
Rainy Day Supply, 888-412-3434, www.cyberatl.net/~rdsupply
Ready Made Resources, 800-627-3809, www.public.usit.net/robertg
Ready Reserve Foods, 800-453-2202
Safe-Trek Outfitters, 800-424-7870,
   www.montana.avicom.net/safetrek
SamAndy Food & Equipment Co., 800-331-0358
San Francisco Herb Co., 800-227-4530, www.sfherb.com
Star Kitchen Ranch Brand Products, 800-882-6325
Survivor Industries, 805-498-6062
These Times, 518-392-2886, www.TheseTimes.com

U.S. Calvary, 888-888-7228, 800-777-7172, www.uscav.com
Van Drunen Farms, 815-472-3100
Walton Feed Inc., 800-847-0465, www.waltonfeed.com

Gold/Silver/Investments
Centennial Precious Metals, 800-869-5115, www.usagold.com
Dallas Gold & Silver Exchange, 800-527-5307, www.dgse.com
Dallas Precious Metals, 888-380-6661,
    www.dallaspreciousmetals.com
Double Eagle Investments, 800-290-4127
Resource Consultants Inc., 800-494-4149
Southwest Trading Diversities, 800-810-4456
Strategic Commodity Trading, 800-437-7370,
    www.strategictraders.com

Health/First-aid Kits
American Products Corp., 503-672-7502,
    www.americanfamilynetwork.com
Common Sense Products, 800-346-0368, www.npwt.net/~comsense
JRH Enterprises, 904-797-9462, www.logoplex.com/resources/jrh
Nitro-Pak Preparedness Center, 800-866-4876, www.nitro-pak.com
Ready Made Resources, 800-627-3809, www.public.usit.net/robertg

Home Schooling
American Products Corp., 503-672-7502,
    www.americanfamilynetwork.com
Calvert School, 410-243-6030, www.calvertschool.org
Clonlara School, 800-200-6163, www.clonlara.org
Common Sense Products, 800-346-0368, www.npwt.net/~comsense
Covenant Home Curriculum, 414-781-2171,
    www.covenanthome.com
CyberSchool, 541-687-6939, www.CyberSchool.4j.lane.edu
Family Learning Services, 541-998-5735, www.fls-homeschool.com
Home Study International, 800-782-4769, www.hsi.edu
Keystone National High School, 800-255-4937,
    www.keystonehighschool.com
LPH Resource Center, www.netaxs.com/~rmk/lph.html
Michael Olaf Co., 707-826-1557,
    www.members.aol.com/Michaelola/montessori.html

New College of Norwich University, 802-828-8855,
    www.norwich.edu/newcollege
Oak Meadow School, 802-387-2021, www.oakmeadow.com
Sycamore Tree Center for Home Education, 800-779-6750,
    www.sycamoretree.com
West River Academy, 800-400-1528 ext. 2848, WRU2420@aol.com

Power

Generators

American Products Corp., 503-672-7502,
    www.americanfamilynetwork.com
China Diesel Imports, 619-669-1995, www.chinadiesel.com
Lehman's, 330-857-5757, www.lehmans.com
Nitro-Pak Preparedness Center, 800-866-4876, www.nitro-pak.com
Northern Tools & Power, 800-533-5545, www.northern-online.com
Ready Made Resources, 800-627-3809, www.public.usit.net/robertg
Real Goods, 800-762-7325, www.realgoods.com

Solar Power

Backwoods Solar, 208-263-4290, wwww.backwoodssolar.com
Delivered Solutions, 800-929-0448, www.deliveredSolutions.com
EMI, 888-MR-SOLAR, www.emi4solar.com
Real Goods, 800-762-7325, www.realgoods.com
Sierra Solar, 800-51-SOLAR, www.sierrasolar.com
Solar Electric, 800-842-5678, www.solarelectric.com

Wind Power

Delivered Solutions, 800-929-0448, www.deliveredSolutions.com
Kansas Wind Power, 785-364-4407, www.smallfarm.com/kanswind
Real Goods, 800-762-7325, www.realgoods.com
Sierra Solar, 800-51-SOLAR, www.sierrasolar.com
Southwest Windpower, 520-779-9463, www.windenergy.com
WinGen 2000, 760-945-9360, www.wingen2000.com

Survival Resources

Clothes, camping equipment, first-aid kits, toilets, et cetera
B&A Products, 918-696-5998, www.baproducts.com

BayGen Power USA, 800-WIND-234, www.freeplay.pair.com
  (radios)
Brigade Quartermasters, 800-338-4327, www.actiongear.com
  (tactical)
Cabela's, 800-237-4444, www.cabelas.com *(clothing, outdoors items)*
Campmor, 800-226-7667, www.campmor.com
Cheaper Than Dirt, 888-625-3848, www.cheaperthandirt.com
Common Sense Products, 800-346-0368, www.npwt.net/~comsense
Country Store & Kitchen Specialties, 800-896-9131,
  www.HealthyHarvest.com
Eagle Industries, 314-343-7547, www.eagleindustries.com *(tactical)*
Emergency Essentials, 800-999-1863, www.beprepared.com
Firequest, 870-881-8688, www.firequest.com *(firearms accessories)*
JRH Enterprises, 904-797-9462, www.logoplex.com/resources/jrh
LifeLink, 800-543-3457, www.lifelink.com
L.L. Bean, 800-221-4221, www.llbean.com *(clothing, outdoor items)*
Major Surplus & Survival, 800-441-8855,
  www.MajorSurplusNSurvival.com
Maple Leaf Industries, 800-671-5323, www.mapleleafinc.com
Nitro-Pak Preparedness Center, 800-866-4876, www.nitro-pak.com
Preparedness Mart, 800-773-0437, www.preparednessmart.com
Rainy Day Supply, 888-412-3434, www.cyberatl.net/~rdsupply
Ready Made Resources, 800-627-3809, www.public.usit.net/robertg
REI, 800-426-4840, www.rei.com *(clothing, outdoor items)*
Safe-Trek Outfitters, 800-424-7870,
  www.montana.avicom.net/safetrek
U.S. Calvary, 888-888-7228, 800-777-7172, uscav.com *(military,*
  outdoor items)

Water Resources

Purification, filters, containers, et cetera
American Products Corp., 503-672-7502,
  www.americanfamilynetwork.com
Campmor, 800-226-7667, www.campmor.com
JRH Enterprises, 904-797-9462, www.logoplex.com/resources/jrh
Katadyn Water Purifiers, 800-543-9124

Major Surplus & Survival, 800-441-8855,
    www.MajorSurplusNSurvival.com
New Millennium Concepts, 888-778-5279
Nitro-Pak Preparedness Center, 800-866-4876, www.nitro-pak.com
Preparedness Plus, 888-839-0334, www.enol.com~preplus
Ready Made Resources, 800-627-3809, www.public.usit.net/robertg
REI, 800-426-4840, www.rei.com
U.S. Calvary, 888-888-7228, 800-777-7172, www.uscav.com
Watertanks.com, 877-420-8657, www.watertanks.com

Information Resources

Web Sites

Computer Related

These listings take you to Y2K-related pages at various computer companies.

Acer
www.acer.com.tw/service/y2k

Adobe
www.adobe.com/newsfeatures/year2000/prodlist.html

Apple Computers
www.apple.com/macos/info/2000.html

Borland
www.inprise.com/devsupport/y2000/productlist.html

Corel
www.corel.com/2000.htm

Dell
www.support.dell.com/support

Gateway
www.gateway.com

Hewlett-Packard
www.hp.com/year2000

Intuit
www.intuit.com/support

Iomega
www.iomega.com/company/y2k.html

Lotus
www.lotus.com/home.nsf/tabs/y2k

Micron
www.support.micronpc.com

Microsoft Year 2000 Resource Center
    www.microsoft.com/technet/topics/year2k/default.htm
National Software Testing Laboratory
    www.nstl.com/html/nstl_y2k.html
Oracle
    www.oracle.com/year2000/2000/2000.htm
Tandem
    www.tandem.com/year2000/y2kcpinf/Y2KCPINF.htm

Government Agencies

These sites contain general information about each agency and the services it provides to the public. Many of these sites also have dedicated pages on the year 2000 issue that warrant your attention.

Centers for Disease Control and Prevention
    www.cdc.gov
Central Fund of Canada
    www.centralfund.com
Defense Information Systems Agency
    www.disa.mil/cio/y2k/cioosd.html
Federal Emergency Management Agency
    www.fema.gov
Federal Financial Institutions Examination Council
    www.ffiec.gov/y2k/default.htm
Federal Reserve Board
    www.bog.frb.fed.us/y2k
Federal Y2K Office
    www.y2k.gov
Food and Drug Administration
    www.fda.gov
General Accounting Office
    www.gao.gov/y2k.htm
General Services Administration
    www.itpolicy.gsa.gov
National Weather Service
    www.nws.noaa.gov
President Clinton's Council on the Year 2000 Conversion
    www.y2k.gov

Securities & Exchange Commission
  www.sec.gov/news/studies/yr2000.htm
U.S. Air Force
  www.af.mil
U.S. Army
  www.army.mil
U.S. Department of Agriculture
  www.usda.gov
U.S. House of Representatives
  www.house.gov/~horn
U.S. Navy
  www.doncio.navy.mil/y2k/year2000.htm
U.S. Senate
  www.senate.gov/~bennett
  www.senate.gov/~dodd
  www.senate.gov/~kerry/isy2k.htm
  www.senate.gov/~y2k
U.S. Treasury
  www.treas.gov

Organizations
American Red Cross
  www.redcross.org
American Electricity Reliability Council
  www.nerc.com/~y2k/y2k.html
American Water Works Association
  www.awwa.org/y2ksrvey.htm
Association of Metropolitan Water Agencies
  www.amwa-water.org/y2k/index.html
Cap Gemini America
  www.usa.capgemini.com
Computer Professionals for Social Responsibility
  www.cpsr.org/program/y2k/
Computer Technology Research Corp.
  www.ctrcorp.com/ctrcorp/year2000.html
Gartner Group
  www.gartner.com

Global 2000 Coordinating Group
www.global2k.com
Global Millennium Foundation
www.globalmf.org
Information Technology Association of America
www.itaa.org
ITAA
www.itaa.com
JP Morgan
www.jpmorgan.com/MarketDataInd/Research/Year2000/
index.html
Mitre Corporation
www.mitre.com
Nasir State Research
www.nasire.org/ss/ST2000.html
NERC
www.nerc.com
World Bank Group
www.worldbank.org/y2k
Y2K State Status
www.y2k.com/non-us-fedgov.htm
www.stateside.com/y2k.html
Year 2000 Group
www.wdcy2k.org
Year 2000 Statements—Manufacturers
home-3.worldonline.nl/~vegterda/

Survival

These sites have information and fact sheets on how to prepare and survive adverse weather conditions, such as hurricanes, floods, and severe cold weather. Some also have pages that are dedicated to year 2000 issues.

American Red Cross
www.redcross.org
Cassandra Project
www.cassandraproject.org
Countryside Magazine
www.countrysidemag.com

Federal Emergency Management Agency
www.fema.gov
How-To Survival Documents
forums.cosmoaccess.net/forum/survival/prep/survival.htm
NFSD Disaster Handbook
www.foodsafety.org/dbhome.htm
Survival
www.unidial.com/~sig1/y2k.htm

Y2K Christian Sites

Catholic City!
www.catholicity.com
Christian 2000
www.christian2k.com
Don McAlvany
www.mcalany.com
Pamela O'Riley
www.millennia-bcs.com
Dennis Peacocke
www.scsnet.org
The Power of Prayer
www.y2kprayershield.org
Pat Robertson
www.cbn.com
Jim Rutz
www.openchurch.com
Tim Wilson
www.y2knews.org

Y2K News

These sites compile news articles from around the world on various year 2000 issues. You can stay up-to-date on progress being made to combat the millennium bug by reading these articles.

www.comlinks.com
www.pw2.netcom.com
www.software.year-2000
www.year2000.com/y2karticles.html

www.y2kchaos.com
www.y2kinvestor.com
www.y2knews.com
www.y2knewswire.com
www.y2kreview.com
www.y2ktimebomb.com/Media/index.htm
www.y2ktoday.com
www.headlines.yahoo.com/FC/Tech/Year_2000_Problem

Y2K Web Pages

These Web sites are dedicated to providing daily coverage on the
millennium bug; some are sober and informative while others are
alarmist and inflammatory. They typically post editorials and news
clippings, as well as advice on how to prepare for various disasters.
Many also have bulletin boards and chat rooms where visitors can
post questions and comments about Y2K.

2000 Legal.com
   www.2000legal.com
Karen Anderson's Y2K For Women *(for women only)*
   www.y2kwomen.com
Bridge Information Systems—Y2K News
   www.bridge.com
Cassandra Project
   www.cassandraproject.org
Citizens for Y2K Recovery
   www.y2krecovery.com
Countdown 2000
   www.countdown2000.com
Everything 2000
   www.everything2000.com
Ken Holder Y2K Site
   www.webleyweb.com/y2k/y2k.html
Michael Hyatt Y2K Site
   www.michaelhyatt.com
Peter de Jaeger's Web Site
   www.year2000.com
Tony Keyes Y2K Site
   www.y2kinvestor.com

Jim Lord's Y2K Site
  www.SurviveY2K.com
Millennia
  www.millennia-bcs.com
Mrs. Survival *(for women only)*
  www.mrssurvival.com
Gary North's Y2K Site
  www.garynorth.com
Joseph Project *(for churches and charities)*
  www.josephproject2000.org
The Power of Prayer
  www.y2kprayershield.org
Sangar's Review
  www.y2kreview.com
Support 2000
  www.support2000.com
Bruce F. Webster's Y2K Web Site
  www.bfwa.com/y2k
Westergaard Year 2000
  www.y2ktimebomb.com
Wild 2K
  www.wild2k.com
Tim Wilson's Y2K Web Site
  www.y2knews.com
Ed Yardeni's Y2K Web Site
  www.yardeni.com
Year 2000 Law Center
  www.year2000.com/y2klawcenter.html
Ed Yourdon's Y2K Web Site
  www.yourdon.com
Y2K
  www.y2k.com
Y2K Culture
  www.y2kculture.com
Y2K Links Database
  www.y2klinks.com

Y2K Run
   www.y2krun.com
Y2K Survive
   www.y2ksurvive.com
Y2K Today
   www.y2ktoday.com
Year 2000 *(Peter de Jaeger's site)*
   www.year2000.com
Year 2000 Link Center
   pw2.netcom.com/~helliott/00 frms.html
Year 2000 Problem
   www.erols.com/steve451/impact.htm

Publications

Every family should have a library of books, magazines, and documents on hand that can be referred to in a natural or man-made disaster. *(See Chapter 2 for more details.)* Here are some titles for you to consider. Most can be purchased through a local bookstore, online (www.amazon.com or www.barnesandnoble.com), or through mail order (e.g., Paladin Press, Delta Press).

Food-Related Issues
Barnyard Livestock by Thomas and Looby
The Busy Person's Guide to Preserving Food by Janet Bachand Chadwick
Container Vegetables: The Easy Way to Garden by Sam Cotner
Don't Get Caught with Your Pantry Down! by James Talmage Stevens
The Encyclopedia of Organic Gardening by Rodale Press, Emmaus, PA
Feasting Free on Wild Edibles by Bradford Angier
How to Develop a Low-Cost Family Food-Storage System by Anita Evangelista
MRExcellence Cookbook by Vicki Walters
Root Cellaring: Natural Cold Storage of Fruits and Vegetables by Mike and Nancy Bubel
Square Foot Gardening by Mel Bartholomew

Health and Medicine
Control of Communicable Diseases Manual by Abram S. Benson, American Public Health Association

Disaster Blaster: A Kid's Guide to Being Home Alone by Karin Kasdin and Laura Szabo-Cohen

Ditch Medicine: Advanced Field Procedures for Emergencies by Hugh L. Coffee

Emergency Medical Treatment: Infants, Children and Adults. A Handbook on What to Do in an Emergency to Keep Someone Alive until Help Arrives by Stephen N. Vogel and David H. Manhoff

Heart and Hands: A Midwife's Guide to Pregnancy and Birth by Elizabeth Davis

Help! She's Having a Baby: Emergency Childbirth: A Practical Guide to Help You Know What to Do When It's Up to You by Nancy Crowley

How to Shit in the Woods: An Environmentally Sound Approach to a Lost Art by Kathleen Meyer

The Merck Manual by Robert Berkow, M.D., Editor-in-Chief, Merck Sharp & Dohme Research Laboratories

The Natural Way to Get Well and Stay Well by Dian Buchman

Survival Medicine: Nature's Way by Marilyn Moore

Survivalist's Medicine Chest by Ragnar Benson

U.S. Army Special Forces Medical Handbook (ST 31-91B), Department of the Army

Where There Is No Dentist by Murray Dickson

Where There Is No Doctor by David Werner

The Wordsworth Medical Companion by Susan C. Pescar and Christine A. Nelson, M.D., Wordsworth Editions Ltd.

Magazines

American Journal of Health Communications, published by the National Public Health Information Coalition, Atlanta, GA, 770-458-3811

American Survival Guide, published by McMullen Argus Publishing Inc., Placentia, CA, 714-572-6887

PCNovice Guide to Y2K, published by Sandhills Publishing, Lincoln, NE, 800-733-3809, www.smartcomputing.com

Survival and Preparedness

Boy Scout Handbook published by the Boy Scouts of America

Complete Book of Survival by Ranier Stahlberg

The Emergency-Disaster Survival Guidebook by Mel Deweese

Emergency Survival Communications by Dave Ingram, Universal Electronics

Emergency Survival Packs: How to Prepare 72-Hour and 14-Day Family Evacuation Packs by Blair D. Jaynes

How to Live without Electricity—and Like It by Anita Evangelista

How to Stay Alive in the Woods by Bradford Angier

How to Survive on Land and Sea by Frank C. and John J. Craighead

Living Off the Land by Thomas L. Squier

Living Well on Practically Nothing by Edward H. Romney

Making the Best of Basics by James Talmage Stevens, Old Leaf Press

Preparing for Catastrophe on a Budget by Bruce LaRue

The SAS Urban Survival Guide by John "Lofty" Wiseman

The Sense of Survival by J. Allen South

Skills for Survival: How Families Can Prepare by Esther Dickey

Survival by Chris ar.d Gretchen Janowsky

Survival (FM 21-76), June 1992, Department of the Army Field Manual

Survival: 17 Ways to Start a Fire Without a Match and 100 Other Useful Skills by Mel DeWeese, Jim Meuninck, Dr. Bill Forgery and Chris Clark

The Survival Bible by Duncan Long

The Survival Retreat: A Total Plan for Retreat Defense by Ragnar Benson

Surviving Doomsday by C. Bruce Sibley

The Trapper's Bible: Traps, Snares and Pathguards by Dale Martin

The U.S. Armed Forces Survival Manual edited by John Boswell, Times Books

Notice:

Delta Press Ltd., Paladin Press, and Cheaper Than Dirt publish a slew of survival, self-defense, firearms, military science, and homesteading books. (Warning: Some titles are quite liberal/extremist in their approach.) To request a catalogue:

Cheaper Than Dirt (888-625-2506, www.cheaperthandirt.com)
Delta Press Ltd. (870-862-4984, www.deltapress.com)

Paladin Press (303-443-7250, www.paladin-press.com)
Another source of survival books is Major Surplus & Survival:
800-441-8855 (www.MajorSurplusNSurvival.com)

Year 2000

A Business Guide to the Year 2000 by Lynn Craig and Mike Kusmirak
Finding and Fixing Your Year 2000 Problem: A Guide For Small Businesses and Organizations by Jesse Feiler and Barbara Butler
The Millennium Bug: How to Survive the Coming Chaos by Michael S. Hyatt
Surviving the Y2K Crisis by Jim Lord
Surviving Y2K by Boston T. Party
Time Bomb 2000: What the Year 2000 Computer Crisis Means to You! by Edward and Jennifer Yourdon
The Upside of Y2K by Judy Laddon, Tom Atlee and Larry Shook
The Year 2000 Computer Crisis: An Investor's Survival Guide by Tony Keyes
The Year 2000 Software Crisis: Challenge of the Century by William M. Ulrich and Ian S. Hayes
The Y2K Computer Crash Scenario by Dr. John Mrozek, Paladin Press
The Y2K Survival Guide by Bruce F. Webster, Prentice-Hall
What Will Become of Us? Counting Down to Y2K by Julian Gregori
Y2K for Women: How to Protect Your Home and Family in the Coming Crisis by Karen Anderson (self-published, order via www.y2kwomen.com)
Year 2000: Personal Protection Guide by J.R. Morris
Year 2000 Recession? by Dr. Ed Yardeni
Y2K Crisis by Donald S. McAlvany

Weaponscraft

Armed and Female by Paxton Quigley
Justifiable Homocide: The Intelligent Use of Deadly Force by Denny Hansen
Self-Defense Requires No Apologies by Jan Jones
The Rights of Gun Owners by Alan M. Gottlieb
Traveler's Guide to the Firearm Laws of the Fifty States by J. Scott Kappas, Esq.

Local Resources

There are a number of resources in your own community that you can approach for information about a variety of topics pertaining to the millennium bug. The organizations listed here typically have brochures, fact sheets and other documents that you can put to good use. Use your telephone directory to find the agency's address and phone number.

American Red Cross Chapter
Boy Scouts of America
Cooperative Extension
4-H Club
Girl Scouts of America
library
state government
    Agriculture
    Emergency Management
    Environmental Services
    Health and Human Services

About the Author

S. F. Tomajczyk is the founder and managing editor of the award-winning magazine, *The American Journal of Health Communications*, which is published by the National Public Health Information Coalition (Atlanta, GA). He served eight years with the New Hampshire Division of Public Health Services as a public information officer, where he was involved in a variety of health-related crisis issues, including disease outbreaks, water-sanitation issues, product recalls, radiation hazards, and natural and man-made disasters.

A graduate of the University of Michigan, Steve is trained in crisis communications, emergency management, first aid, wilderness survival, and the Incident Command System. He is also familiar with Federal Emergency Plan D—America's continuity-of-government response plan—and he is an acknowledged expert on terrorism and security issues. He is listed in *Contemporary Authors* and *Who's Who in America*.